THE ART OF LIGHTING

An International Profile of Home Lighting

First published in the United States of America by
Rockport Publishers, Inc.
33 Commercial Street
Gloucester, Massachusetts 01930-5089
Telephone: (978) 282-9590
Facsimile: (978) 283-2742
www.rockpub.com

ISBN 1-56496-707-7

10 9 8 7 6 5 4 3 2

Design: Benchmark Productions, Boston, Massachusetts
Front cover photos left: Sharon Risedorph, (credits appear on page 23);
    right: Tuca Reins, (credits appear on page 85),
Back cover photos: Douglas A. Salin, top, (credits appear on page 35);
    Robert Ames Cook, bottom, (credits appear on page 150)
Page 4 photo by John Sutton, lighting design by Duane Johnson
    (credits appear on page 64)
Page 6 photo by Douglas A. Salin, lighting design by Linda Ferry
    (credits appear on page 68)

Printed in China.

DEDICATION

This book is dedicated to my family and
to my family of friends who fill my life
with love and purpose. They are the
mirror by which I see myself.

ACKNOWLEDGMENTS

Putting together a book like this takes
a tremendous number of talented and
generous people. I would like to thank
all of the designers and architects who
contributed their fine work, along with
the photographers who so skillfully
captured the magic of these projects.
These people know the value of teamwork.

My heartfelt appreciation goes out to Tim
Brace and Steve Rao, without whose help
and emotional support this book would
not have come together.

I would also like to thank Pat and Lawrie
Fambrini, who took me under their wings
when I first came to San Francisco and
made me feel that I was home at last.

THE ART OF LIGHTING

An International Profile of Home Lighting

Randall Whitehead

ROCKPORT

CONTENTS

INTRODUCTION
THE INCREDIBLE IMPACT OF LIGHTING

Nothing has a greater impact on a home than lighting, because illumination affects us on so many levels. Lighting influences the appearance, tone, and impression of every single object or space in a house through how it is lighted. It can make or break the overall ambiance of a residential interior.

Yet all too often, people add it as an afterthought – "Oh yes, let's also do some lighting" – after the architecture has been laid out and construction has begun. This is a huge mistake. Along with all the other design components, lighting needs to be considered at the beginning of the design process. Homeowners, especially, need to learn at least the basics about lighting design so they can contribute to important decisions about lighting their residences. Unfortunately, too many architects, interior designers, and contractors have had little training in this specialty.

Many new technologies have emerged during the past decade,

making knowing the fundamentals of lighting design more necessary than ever. Who needed lighting expertise when the only thing available was a ceiling socket and a light bulb? Today, however, homeowners can choose from a tremendous variety of luminaires (a "luminaire" is a complete fixture, including all parts necessary for positioning and obtaining power supply). Fluorescent lighting alone has gone through a revolutionary shift, and, with energy considerations and construction codes, is now a "must" for the home.

People also have changed the way they live and entertain. Many houses are designed with an open plan, encouraging movement from

space to space. New entertainment centers and control systems also have changed the way people use their houses. Well-done lighting design takes into account all of these needs and styles of living.

The Functions of Illumination

When planning residential lighting, focus on layering various types of lighting to accommodate the three elements that need illumination: people, architecture, and key objects such as art and collectibles. While all of these elements are important, the most critical consideration is lighting the people who will use the space.

Ambient: Soft General Illumination to Humanize a Space   Ambient lighting fills a room with a gentle, inviting overall glow that humanizes the space. To create good fill light, modern lighting design bounces illumination off walls and ceilings so the lighting is sensed only after being reflected. Thus glare and bright spots are avoided, and the light is flattering because it doesn't cast harsh shadows on people's faces. Ambient lighting may come from wall sconces, torchieres, or uplights mounted over cabinets, columns, or beams.

Decorative: Luminaires That Create Sparkle   The job of decorative luminaires, such as chandeliers, lanterns, and candlestick-type wall brackets, is to add shimmering texture and give the illusion of providing the room's ambient illumination. However, this type of lighting must be supported by a well-designed layer of supplementary lighting, since

decorative luminaires cannot be the source of overall illumination without overpowering the space.

Accent: Lighting That Highlights   Accent lighting uses carefully focused beams to illuminate an object, artwork, planting, or architectural detail. Artistic effect is a primary goal. Often, accent lighting is designed to make the viewer think the illumination is provided by a source that really does not provide much lighting at all, such as a candle or chandelier. Accent lighting can be provided by recessed adjustable luminaires, track lighting, or portable luminaires.

Task: Fixtures Geared for Work   Task lighting is the tightly focused, unobstructed, intense light needed where people do work or other activities requiring close scrutiny. Task lighting generally is provided by such luminaires as pharmacy-style lamps, tabletop lamps, under-cabinet strip lighting, or, in bathrooms, vertical strip lighting flanking the mirrors.

ENTRANCES

PORTALS TO THE HEART OF A HOME

Just as you judge a person by your first impression, you judge a home by what you see and sense at the entry.

As guests approach a house in the evening, outside lighting should create a welcoming impression. The house number should be lit, and cues indicating which way to approach and enter should be provided.

Inside the home, create an inviting atmosphere by layering the light. First, infuse the entry with ambient illumination. Fill light is especially important in this area, since gentle illumination helps people feel at ease in a new setting. Make sure the walls and ceiling aren't too dark for indirect light to be reflected and diffused effectively throughout the space.

Avoid the common error of relying on only one source of entrance illumination such as a decorative luminaire centered on the ceiling. A chandelier, for instance, will draw all the attention and

overpower the space. As you greet guests, you will end up in silhouette. Instead, install a good source of ambient light so that a chandelier can be dimmed to a subtle sparkle.

Naturally, accent lighting also should be part of the design. Using spots of illumination to highlight a dramatic painting, sculpture, or architectural detail can arouse guests' anticipation of what's to come as they explore the rest of the house.

Creating Illusion Through Lighting

Entrances come in all shapes and sizes, but by using lighting and

related design techniques you can redefine the envelope of the space. First, decide on your desired outcome. Do you want the entrance to look larger or more intimate? Do you want it to dazzle or to exude homey comfort?

If your entrance area is cramped, for example, you may be able to use illusion and lighting to visually "steal" an area of another room and make it seem part of the entrance. Directing accent lighting onto a sculpture, flower arrangement, or painting visible in an adjacent room helps make that area seem part of the entry. Techniques utilizing mirrors and glass blocks also can make entrances seem larger. If the entrance illumination does not adequately light the ceiling, it

The chandelier in this grand entry is dimmed to a glow, while recessed fixtures focus on the art and flowers.

Lighting and Interior Design: J. Hettinger Interiors
Architecture: Barry Holloway
Photo: Doug Johnson

not only makes the room seem small but neglects what often can be wonderful decorative elements in a design. Beams, coffers, moldings, ceiling frescoes, and other well-lit design components can become marvelous details, visually expanding the space upward and giving people something to engage their interest as they enter. When illuminated, stairways in an entrance also make the area seem larger and provide another focus for guests' attention. Lighting a painting on the stairway wall, or plants or sculpture on a stair landing, also helps a small entry assume the appearance of a grander entrance hall.

(Overleaf) Cove lighting is integrated into the architectural detail of the house. Recessed downlights emphasize the columns.

Lighting and Interior Design: J. Hettinger Interiors
Photo: Doug Johnson

The well-proportioned entry invites people to the windows and the sea beyond. Uplighting of the structural beams adds a sense of solidity.

Lighting Design and Architecture: Lucky Bennett
Interior Design: Peggy Chestnut
Photo: Russell Abraham

A series of torch-like wall sconces mounted on the wood beams invite guests into the various rooms off the entrance.

Lighting Design: Randall Whitehead, IALD,
    and Catherine Ng, IES
Interior Design: Carol Saal
Architecture: Stan Field
Photo: Dennis Anderson

The shaded chandelier and candlestick wall sconces seem to provide all the room's illumination. In reality, the Roman bust and console table are highlighted with miniature recessed adjustable fixtures made especially for remodeling projects.

Lighting Design: Randall Whitehead, IALD,
    and Catherine Ng, IES
Interior Design: Christian Wright
Photo: Dennis Anderson

A copper luminaire swoops down from the ceiling to provide accent lighting through a sculptural medium.

Lighting Design:
    Randall Whitehead, IALD,
    and Catherine Ng, IES
Interior Design: Carol Saal
Architecture: Stan Field
Photo: Dennis Anderson

A recessed framing projector casts an intriguing pattern of light

onto the fluted wall detail. A pair of recessed low-voltage

fixtures bounces light off the ball-capped newel post.

Lighting Design: Craig Roeder, IALD
Interior Design: Loyd Ray Taylor and Charles Paxton Gremillion
Photo: Robert Ames Cook

A mirror ball tucked behind the cap of the carved chest

adds a touch of theater to this entryway.

Lighting Design: Randall Whitehead, IALD,
 and Catherine Ng, IES
Interior Design: Randall Whitehead
Photo: Dennis Anderson

Well lighting mounted in the floor at the base of the two

pedestals casts intricate shadows onto the vaulted ceiling.

Lighting Design: Craig Roeder, IALD
Interior Design: Loyd Ray Taylor and Charles Paxton Gremillion
Architecture: Hendricks & Wall
Photo: Robert Ames Cook

The refraction off the clock onto the wall adds an amazing multidimensionality to this entrance hall. Uplights softly highlight the architectural detailing of the columns and a chest that once belonged to Marie Antoinette.

Lighting Design: Craig Roeder, IALD
Interior Design: Loyd Ray Taylor and Charles Paxton Gremillion
Architecture: Hendricks & Wall
Photo: Robert Ames Cook

Indirect lighting along the circumference of the dome detail highlights the silver leaf finish. Recessed low-voltage luminaires add visual interest to the center table and clock.

Lighting Design: Barbara Bouyea, IALD, IES
Interior Design and Architecture: Mil Bodron
Photo: Ira Montgomery

Cove lighting along this incredible entry's coffered ceiling keeps the architectural detailing from being lost. The magnificent chandelier hides an indirect halogen source that brings the crystals to life and provides additional ambient light.

Lighting Design:
    Barbara Bouyea, IALD, IES
Interior Design:
    Bobbie Dawn Lander
Architecture:
    Richard Drummond Davis
Photo: Ira Montgomery

A pair of art-glass sconces flank this entrance area. Lighting in the living room draws the eye, with recessed adjustable luminaires accenting the coromandel screen and coffee table.

Lighting and Interior Design: McDonald & Moore, Ltd.
Architecture: Duncan Todd, AIA
Photo: David Livingston

Indirect lighting incorporated into corbel-like wall sconces illuminates the groin-vault ceiling. Recessed adjustable accent lighting focuses on the art and flowers.

Lighting Design: Barbara Bouyea, IALD, IES
Interior Design: Bobbie Dawn Lander
Architecture: Richard Drummond Davis
Photo: Ira Montgomery

The custom tabletop and pendant luminaires by Ahnalisa Moore lend an amber glow to the entrance's wood surfaces in this mountain home.

Lighting Design: Ahnalisa Moore
Interior Design: Maria Tenglia
Architecture: Gary Francis & Assoc.
Photo: Scott Zimmerman

The illuminated ceiling detail creates a center of light that draws visitors into the entry. Recessed fixtures highlight the greenery.

Lighting/Interior Design and Architecture: Gordon Stein
Photo: Douglas A. Salin

The eclectic collection of modern art is vividly illuminated with recessed adjustable low-voltage fixtures, giving this entry the ambience of a gallery space.

Lighting Design: Randall Whitehead, IALD, ASID
   Affiliate, and Catherine Ng, IES
Interior Design: Diane Chapman
Architecture: Mark Thomas, AIA
Photo: Michael Bruk, Photo/Graphics

A simple wall evenly illuminated with a wash of light becomes a massive, quiet canvas in the entrance to this San Francisco residence. Recessed fixtures provide additional illumination without sacrificing the view of the bay.

Lighting Design: Becca Foster IES, DLF
Architecture: Lewis Butler
Photo: Sharon Risedorph

Three looping light fixtures turn accent light into art

itself. A metal wall sconce adds a balance of fill light to

this entry.

Lighting Design and Architecture: Dan Phipps, AIA
Photo: John Sutton

Plaster wall sconces enhance the vaulted ceiling of this

entry hall in a home in the Grand Cayman Islands.

Lighting/Interior Design and Architecture: Kathleen Buoymaster
Photo: Dennis Anderson

A cut-crystal surface-mounted luminaire projects an

intriguing pattern of refracted light. The painting is

illuminated by a slim-profile halogen picture light.

Lighting and Interior Design: Kathleen Buoymaster
Photo: Dennis Anderson

When visible from an entry hall, a well-lit stairway

can give the impression of added openness and grandeur.

Here, hidden low-voltage incandescent strip lighting

brings out the stairway's sculptural shape.

Lighting Design:
    Charles K. Thompson, AIA, IALD, IESNA, and
    Sarah J. Gibson, IESNA, IALD
Interior Design: Jere Cavanaugh
Architecture: J. B. Johnson
Photo: Charles K. Thompson

The goal of the lighting was to use custom decorative fixtures made of period materials to support the architectural style, which is a blend of Mediterranean and California Mission. Supplemental lighting is provided by a variety of energy-efficient sources.

Lighting Design: Alan Lindsley, AIA, IESNA, Lindsley-McCoy Architecture and Lighting
Architecture: Richard Bartlett, AIA
Photo: Dennis Anderson

A center row of recessed fixtures leads people from the entry into the rest of the house. A framing projector illuminates the Georgia O'Keefe painting at the end of the hall. Lighting beyond the windows offers a glimpse of the pool area.

Lighting Design: Randall Whitehead, IALD, ASID Affiliate, and Catherine Ng, IES
Interior Design: Helen C. Reuter
Photo: Douglas A. Salin

Simplicity is the key word in this Asian-inspired interior. Low-voltage track fixtures mounted on the sides of the apex beam dramatize the orchids and flower arrangement. Lighting above the divider walls softly illuminates the ceiling structure.

Lighting and Interior Design: Carla Carstens, ASID, CID
Architecture: Michael Helm
Photo: Douglas A. Salin

LIVING ROOMS

BLENDING DRAMA WITH VERSATILITY

In the past, living rooms seemed to be off limits except when entertaining company. Nowadays, though, living rooms aren't just reserved for special occasions. As the old "hands-off" formality softens, living room furniture is becoming more comfortable, its arrangement more relaxed. Furniture plans also are less static, with decorative items rotated around the house to keep the look fresh. Thus lighting should be as flexible as the rest of the home's components, and it needs to satisfy a variety of needs. Lighting for entertaining in the living room is important, but your main concern should be adequate illumination for day-to-day activities.

Overall Lighting

The first way to make your living room more inviting is to provide adequate ambient light. Perhaps the easiest alternative is flanking the fireplace with torchieres. A better solution–one that provides illumination that's more even–is four wall sconces.

If your living room has a 9-foot (2.7-meter) or higher ceiling, you have additional options. Pendant luminaires with an overall length of 2 to 2 1/2 feet (.6 to .8 meters) work well for a 9- to 12-foot-high (2.7- to 3.7-meter-high) flat ceiling. Pitched ceilings require luminaires adapted for the slope.

A higher ceiling also works well in conjunction with cove lighting, where the light source is hidden behind a crown molding or valence. In living rooms with gabled ceilings and support beams parallel to the floor, linear strip lighting can be mounted on top of the beams to create ambient light.

Focusing Light for Effect

Once fill light is provided, the next consideration is accent lighting. Remember that the type of luminaire chosen for accent lighting should be flexible. As you move furniture and art, the lighting needs to be able to accommodate new arrangements.

Recessed Lighting   Recessed adjustable luminaires are excellent for accent lighting. In new construction and remodeling projects, think about possible furniture arrangements before designing the lighting, since placement depends on what might be highlighted. In an existing residence that already has recessed luminaires, you can increase

flexibility by leaving the housing (the main part of a recessed luminaire installed inside the ceiling) and replacing the trim (the visible part of a recessed unit, attached to the housing) with line- or low-voltage adjustable versions.

Track Lighting   Use track lighting when other options aren't available. For example, if the ceiling depth is inadequate for housing recessed luminaires, then a surface-mounted system must be used. In living rooms, track lighting works best in a perimeter run. Installing molding on either side of the track helps integrate the system with the architecture.

Halogen Bridge Systems   An alternative to recessed and track lighting is a relatively new product, generically called a halogen bridge or cable system. This low-voltage setup runs two parallel wires across a ceiling space. Accent luminaires are then clipped and locked into place along the wires.

Task Lighting

Finally, plan the task lighting. Think about what you'll be doing in the living room, from reading to watching television to playing cards or board games. If you're building a new house and want to place furniture in the middle of the room, remember to specify floor plugs so cords don't cross the floor to a wall outlet.

A whimsical wall sconce provides a glow of warm light, while recessed, adjustable, low-voltage fixtures gently highlight the tablescape.

Lighting Design: Randall
    Whitehead, IALD, ASID
    Affiliate and Catherine Ng,
    IES
Interior Design: Jessica Hall &
    Associates
Photo: Dennis Anderson

(Overleaf) Recessed adjustable low-voltage luminaires illuminate the many fine art objects in this richly detailed Dallas residence. The highly adjustable system allows lights to be repositioned when items are moved to new locations.

Lighting Design: Craig Roeder, IALD
Interior Design: Loyd Ray Taylor and
    Charles Paxton Gremillion
Photo: Robert Ames Cook

Recessed small-aperature fixtures subtly highlight the art and tabletops, allowing the candles to give the illusion of providing the illumination.

Lighting Design: Randall Whitehead, IALD, ASID Affiliate
    and Catherine Ng, IES
Interior Design: Jessica Hall & Associates
Photo: Dennis Anderson

Recessed accent lights make a dramatic statement for a pair of sitting Buddha figures.

Lighting Design: Randall Whitehead, IALD, ASID Affiliate
    and Catherine Ng, IES
Interior Design: Jessica Hall & Associates
Photo: Dennis Anderson

Recessed adjustable fixtures with mirror reflectors

accent the art in the room. Uplighting behind the palm

casts graceful shadows on the ceiling.

Lighting Design: Linda Ferry, IES, ASID Affiliate
Interior Design: John Schneider
Architecture: William David Martin, AIA
Photo: Douglas A. Salin

Recessed fixtures mounted alongside the skylight

create an island of light in the seating area. Track

fixtures accent art and plants.

Lighting Design: Linda Ferry, IES, ASID Affiliate
Architecture: David Allen Smith
Photo: Douglas A. Salin

Recessed adjustable low-voltage

luminaires set at an acute angle

bring out the texture of the stone

wall, while well-hidden indirect

lighting enhances the wood ceiling.

Lighting Design: Linda Ferry, IES,
    ASID Affiliate
Interior Design:
    Winifred Dell'Ario
Architecture:
    George Brook-Kothlow
Photo: Douglas A. Salin

The reading lamp's opaque copper shade projects light downward, keeping the brightness from interfering with the room's overall ambiance.

A handcrafted pendant fixture by Christina Spann helps set the mood in this Tuscany-style living room. Indirect cove lighting shows off the ceiling detail while adding ambient light. Exterior lighting visually opens up the room.

Lighting Design: Catherine Ng, IES, and
    Randall Whitehead, IALD, ASID Affiliate
Interior Design: Jessica Hall & Associates
Photo: Dennis Anderson

Display niches on either side of the fireplace use 50-watt halogen recessed fixtures to show off treasures.

*In a residence done in Mediterranean Spanish style,
the open-beam ceiling made the living room seem dark
and oppressive. The solution: custom-designed sconces
that humanize the space by creating a secondary
ceiling line, and low-profile track fixtures by Capri
that illuminate the palms and coffee table.*

Lighting Design: Linda Ferry, IES, ASID Affiliate
Interior Design: Dudley Williams
Architecture: Rollen E. Stringham
Photo: Douglas A. Salin

*Indirect lighting along the side
walls adds a subtle glow to the
sloped ceiling. A few well-placed
monopoint luminaires highlight
the table.*

Lighting and Interior Design:
    Lindy Smallwood
Photo: Doug Johnson

Indirect cove lighting and recessed adjustable fixtures

work together to create a cohesive, comfortable

environment.

Lighting and Interior Design: J. Hettinger Interiors
Photo: Doug Johnson

This very traditional setting uses just a few recessed fixtures to accent the tapestry, allowing the wall sconces and table lamps to appear to be the room's sources of illumination.

Lighting Design: Alfredo Zaparolli
Interior Design: Eugene Anthony
Photo: John Vaughan

At night, well-placed fixtures illuminate the living room of this mountain retreat. A flexible system tucked between the beams provides accent lighting, while the warm glow of the mica table lamp and roaring fire invite people in.

Lighting and Interior Design: William David Martin
Photo: Douglas A. Salin

Recessed adjustable fixtures highlight the coromandel screen, art, and flowers. Table lamps add an intimate ambiance without overpowering the surroundings.

Lighting and Interior Design:
   Donald Maxcy, ASID
Photo: Russell Abraham

Custom wall sconces made of rusticated metal and fiberglass offer a rough contrast to the clean lines of this Afro-Asian–inspired living room. Recessed adjustable downlights call attention to the art, while lighting on the deck allows a gargoyle face to barely emerge from the shadows.

Lighting Design: Randall Whitehead, IALD,
  and Catherine Ng, IES
Interior Design: Randall Whitehead
Photo: Dennis Anderson

This cozy setting seems to draw all its light from the fire and table lamps. In reality, three recessed adjustable fixtures are illuminating the center table and the ivy-filled urn. Opaque lamp shades keep the portable luminaires from visually overpowering the room.

Lighting Design: Randall Whitehead, IALD,
  and Catherine Ng, IES
Interior Design: Christian Wright
Photo: Dennis Anderson

Recessed accent lights show off the art and art objects without interfering with the traditional style of the interior design and architecture.

Lighting Design:
  Barbara Bouyea, IALD, IES
Interior Design:
  Bobbie Dawn Lander
Architecture:
  Richard Drummond Davis
Photo: Ira Montgomery

A series of halogen wall sconces with asymmetrical

reflectors fill this striking room with soft illumination.

Recessed adjustable downlights bring focus to the art

and artifacts, while recessed lighting above the

shelving shows off smaller collected items.

Lighting Design: Barbara Bouyea, IALD, IES
Interior Design: Cheri Etchelecu
Architecture: Bill Booziotis/Holly Hall, Booziotis & Co.
Photo: Ira Montgomery

Halogen track heads uplight the ceiling from the trestle-style beams, while additional heads highlight art and furniture.

Lighting and Interior Design:
  Ruth Soforenko, ASID
Photo: Russell Abraham

The lighting design emphasizes the theatrical essence of this residence. The use of colored gels contributes to the visual excitement, and the plants' hidden uplighting adds dimension.

Lighting and Interior Design: Lynn Augstein
Photo: Douglas A. Salin

This residence's open floor plan was carefully

considered by the lighting designer, who balanced

individual spaces within the overall composition.

Contemporary light sources work in concert with

traditional fixtures.

Lighting Design: Linda Ferry, IES, ASID Affiliate
Interior Design: Marilyn Riding
Architecture: Ravi Varma
Photo: Douglas A. Salin

Rhythmic highlighting of the art on the thick, cream-colored fresco walls creates soft reflective illumination throughout the room.

Lighting Design: Linda Ferry, IES, ASID Affiliate
Architecture: Lee von Hasseln
Photo: Philip Harvey

This design uses the best in modern lighting
technology while avoiding the use of chandeliers,
sconces, and table lamps. Fixtures were selected for
their low ceiling impact.

Lighting Design: Linda Ferry, IES, ASID Affiliate
Interior Design: John Newcomb
Architecture: Stephen Wilmot
Photo: Philip Harvey

In the remodeling of this house, existing recessed trims
were replaced by trims with a smaller opening, creating
less ceiling impact and reducing awareness of the
source of light.

Lighting Design: Linda Ferry, IES, ASID Affiliate
Interior Design: Beatrice Krell
Photo: Philip Harvey

The lighting in this living room is controlled by a pre-set programmable dimming system. Notice how the blue painting is framed with light, creating the illusion that it is floating on the wall.

Lighting Design: Terry Ohm
Interior Design and Architecture: Mary Ann Schicketanz
Photo: Robert Bengtson

Indirect lighting plays a huge role in emphasizing the dynamic architecture of this Japanese residence.

Lighting Design: Kousaku Matsumoto, IEI Japan
Interior Design: Seiji Tanaka
Architecture: Seiji Tanaka
Photo: Yoshihisa Araki/Toshiya Toyoda.

In this home with twenty-five skylights, evening

illumination was designed to echo the daytime

patterns. Soft lighting and wall washing were

used to spread the light evenly.

Lighting Design: Linda Ferry, IES, ASID Affiliate
Architecture: Lee von Hasseln
Photo: Philip Harvey

Simplicity works its magic in this intimate setting.

Shelf lighting silhouettes books and art objects, an

adjustable recessed downlight focuses on the coffee

table, and two pharmacy lamps offer reading light.

Lighting Design: Becca Foster IES, DLF
Interior Design: Victoria Stone
Photo: Alan Weintraub

An opulent torchiere in the corner adds fill light and

a bit of fantasy to this San Francisco living room.

Recessed adjustable downlights highlight the room's

various features.

Lighting Design: Becca Foster IES, DLF
Interior Design: Victoria Stone
Photo: Alan Weintraub

Lighting located behind the

cobalt blue doors and cap turns

this display case into a piece of

luminous art.

Lighting and Interior Design:
  Joan Malter Osburn
Photo: John Vaughan

By increasing the brightness under the peak of the

living room (above), the designer managed to mimic

the kitchen ceiling's structural design. The reflection

of light on the ceiling (opposite) adds a dimension of

warmth to this house in Vancouver, Canada.

Lighting Design: Janis Huston, IES/IALD
Interior Design: Sherrill Bushfield
Architecture: Eric Stine
Photo: Gary Otte

A "story board" of art is evenly illuminated by a series

of recessed wall wash fixtures.

Lighting Design: Becca Foster IES, DLF
Architecture: Lewis Butler
Photo: Sharon Risedorph

Small rectangular luminaires were mounted on top of support beams for fill light in this home on the east coast of Brazil. Table lamps blend Italian and Japanese styling.

Lighting Design:
  Guinter Parschalk
Interior Design and Architecture:
  Arthur de Mattos Casas
Photo: Tuca Reines

Recessed adjustable low-voltage fixtures bring subtle emphasis to the art collection of this San Francisco home. Wall sconces (not seen in photo) provide the soft fill light.

Lighting Design:
  Randall Whitehead, IALD,
  ASID Affiliate, and
  Catherine Ng, IES
Interior Design: Diane Chapman
Architecture: Mark Thomas, AIA
Photo: Michael Bruk,
  Photo/Graphics

A torchiere works in conjunction with recessed downlighting to produce this gently illuminated space. The subtle light enables the homeowners and their guests to enjoy the outdoor view.

Lighting Design and Architecture
  Dahlin Group
Photo: Doug Johnson

Three coiling snake-like fixtures add to the drama of the living room in this hillside home.

Lighting Design and Architecture: Dan Phipps, AIA
Photo: John Sutton

Plaster wall sconces by Phoenix Day Company are painted to match the wall color. They add ambient light, while a halogen bridge system (not shown) provides accent lighting.

Lighting Design: Catherine Ng, IES, and
    Randall Whitehead, IALD, ASID Affiliate
Interior Design: Joseph Ruggiero & Assoc.
Photo: Russell Abraham

A warm corona of illumination in the ceiling serves as fill light while viewing videos. Recessed fixtures spot objects on the tables, and shelf lighting emphasizes the collection of vessels and figures.

Lighting Design: Craig Roeder, IALD
Interior Design: Duffala/von Thaden Assoc., Inc.
Architecture: Fleischman/Garcia Architects
Photo: Jeff Blanton

single intense pin spot seems to illuminate the

ndelabra from within. Additional recessed fixtures

cus attention on the sculpture and paintings.

ighting Design: Craig Roeder, IALD
nterior Design: Duffala/von Thaden Assoc., Inc.
rchitecture: Fleischman/Garcia Architects
hoto: Jeff Blanton

During the day, this home is bathed in illumination
from skylights; at night, recessed luminaires provide
light.

Interior Design: Priscilla Sanchez, Allied ASID
Architecture: George Sinclair, AIA
Photo: Eric A. Zepeda

This living area's ceiling has no recessed depth,
so fixtures were placed alongside beams to be
unobtrusive. Remote transformers enable the
fixture heads to be as small as possible while
providing light for reading and accenting.

Lighting Design: Duane Johnson, IESNA, CEDIA
Photo: John Sutton

DINING ROOMS

THE MOVEABLE FEAST

Geared for sit-down entertaining for moderate to large groups, dining rooms used to be the last holdout for a traditional static furniture arrangement. After realizing how little time actually was spent formally entertaining at that big table, though, many homeowners have claimed this underutilized room for additional purposes.

To that end, dining room tables have become more flexible in size, folding down to provide more intimate seating for four, or dividing to make a pair of game tables. Even people who still have a large table want to be able to occasionally push it against a wall for buffet dining. All of these changes have set up a need for adjustable lighting and forced homeowners and designers to rethink traditional dining room lighting.

Chandelier Alternatives and Solutions

For eons, the dining room table has been perfectly centered under a chandelier. Now that tables are

moved around, though, centered chandeliers tend to get in the way. Some people who aren't tied to a traditional approach turn to recessed adjustable lighting to provide illumination for the table. For instance, three recessed adjustable luminaires can be used. The middle one highlights the centerpiece. The two outside luminaires cross-illuminate the tabletop itself, adding sparkle to the dishes and silverware. (Make sure the outside luminaires don't point straight down, which would cast harsh shadows on diners and create tabletop glare.) Many homeowners, however, still prefer a chandelier above the table. If you want the flexibility to rearrange furniture but also want traditional lighting, consider the following options:

- Use decorative lighting that hugs the ceiling so the luminaire doesn't look odd when the table is moved.

- Select a pendant light on a pulley system that raises or lowers the luminaire.

- Hang a crystal-type chandelier in a recessed dome so the luminaire's visual relationship is linked to the ceiling configuration rather than the table location.

Getting That Overall Glow

Whichever option you choose for table illumination, don't forget that ambient light also is needed. Torchieres or wall sconces can do the trick. If the dining room has a dome detail, the perimeter can be illuminated so fill light bounces off

the dome's interior. Cove lighting is another excellent source of ambient light. To successfully light a cove, install an even and continuous line of light, preferably from 12- or 24-volt incandescent light rails.

Accenting with Light

If you prefer a traditional dining room chandelier setup, consider adding a recessed adjustable light on either side to add drama to the table. This provides accent lighting for the tabletop and its centerpiece, and also allows the chandelier to be dimmed to a glittering glow while giving the impression of providing the table's illumination. Next, think about lighting for the walls. Instead of illuminating every piece of wall art, allow some items to fall into secondary importance, so they gradually can be discovered by guests. And don't forget to add one or two recessed adjustable luminaires to spotlight the side table, buffet, or console area.

(Overleaf) The sloped ceiling is emphasized by a run of linear low-voltage lighting hidden within the cove detail. Track fixtures highlight the table.

Lighting Design: Linda Ferry, IES, ASID Affiliate
Interior Design: John Newcomb
Architecture: Stephen Wilmot
Photo: Douglas A. Salin

A chandelier and perforated metal, fan-shaped wall sconce add romance to this intimate dining room, and recessed adjustable fixtures illuminate the art and tabletop.

Lighting Design: Randall Whitehead, IALD, ASID Affiliate and Catherine Ng, IES
Interior Design: Jessica Hall & Associates
Photo: J. D. Peterson

Recessed adjustable fixtures add style to a peaceful dining experience. Exterior lighting throws an intriguing shadow pattern on the wall. Votive candles cast a golden glow that adds to the ambience (left).

Lighting Design: Catherine Ng, IES, and Randall Whitehead, IALD, ASID Affiliate
Interior Design: Jessica Hall & Associates
Photo: Dennis Anderson

Contemporary luminaires often blend artistic design with function, as is the case with this opaque pendant by Lightspann and the Mirano glass torchiere.

Lighting and Interior Design:
  Sherry Scott
Photo: John Martin

Recessed adjustable downlights contribute to this dazzling dining room tableau. Votive candles add sparkle without use of a chandelier, while sconces such as the one to the right of the fireplace provide fill light.

Lighting/Interior Design and
  Architecture: Gordon Stein
Photo: Douglas A. Salin

The grouping of cone-shaped pendants becomes a sculptural entity off the dining room table. Wall sconces provide ambient light, while recessed downlights guide people from room to room.

Lighting and Interior Design: Carla Carstens, ASID, CID
Architecture: Michael Helm
Photo: Douglas A. Salin

Fantasy and function blend together to create this intriguing vignette. A circular metal framework supports swags of richly textured fabric as well as the lighting that illuminates the table and art objects.

Lighting Design: Terry Ohm
Interior Design: Bob Miller
Photo: Douglas A. Salin

Lighting within the casework highlights a collection of stemware. Recessed adjustable fixtures are an important aspect of the lighting plan.

Lighting Design: Michael Souter,
    IALD, ASID
Interior Design: Bob Miller,
    Flegels
Photo: Douglas A. Salin

Recessed adjustable low-voltage luminaires draw

attention to the art and tabletop.

Lighting Design: Donald Maxcy, ASID
Interior Design: Bill Reno
Photo: Russell Abraham

Monopoint track fixtures mounted on the side of the

beams illuminate the tabletops. Noguchi lanterns help

humanize the space's scale.

Lighting and Interior Design: Donald Maxcy, ASID
Architecture: Fletcher & Hardoin
Photo: Ron Starr

Recessed downlights illuminate the walls and chandelier of this dining room, while large palms flanking the entrance fall into silhouette.

Lighting and Interior Design: J. Hettinger Interiors
Photo: Doug Johnson

The magnificent sailing ship chandelier gives the illusion of providing the room's illumination, but recessed fixtures actually do the job of highlighting the art and tabletop.

Lighting Design: Linda Ferry, IES, ASID Affiliate
Interior Design: Valera W. Lyles
Photo: Douglas A. Salin

This modern dining room uses wall sconces of forged metal and blown glass to provide ambient illumination. Indirect lighting above the partial wall adds yet another dimension.

Lighting Design: Dahlin Group
Photo: Doug Johnson

A sculptural halogen wire system illuminates the Japanese-style dining area. Recessed adjustable fixtures highlight the owner's collection of art and ceramics.

Lighting and Interior Design: Don Maxcy, ASID
Photo: Russell Abraham

A wonderful grouping of candles and old-style light fixtures adds romance to this dining room. A single recessed accent light highlights the arrangement of spring branches.

Lighting Design: Randall Whitehead, IALD, and
    Catherine Ng, IES
Interior Design: Christian Wright
Photo: Dennis Anderson

A mirror ball used as a centerpiece throws a constellation of starry lights on the walls and ceiling.

Lighting Design: Randall
   Whitehead, IALD, and
   Catherine Ng, IES
Interior Design: Randall
   Whitehead
Photo: Dennis Anderson

A suspended linear triangular-shape luminaire adds fill light to this space, with recessed cans and monopoints providing accent lighting.

Lighting Design: Barbara Bouyea, IALD, IES
Interior Design: Cheri Etchelecu
Architecture: Bill Booziotis and Holly Hall
Photo: Ira Montgomery

The fluted wall is illuminated from behind the matching soffit while the ceiling's recessed adjustable fixtures highlight the table's ziggurat detailing. With a view of the Dallas skyline, this dining room is nothing less than spectacular.

Lighting Design: Craig Roeder, IALD
Interior Design: Loyd Ray Taylor and Charles Paxton Gremillion
Photo: Robert Ames Cook

A combination of sources, from candlelight to concealed accent lights, lends warmth to this large open space. At night, concealed lighting from within the table base adds a unique dimension to this table setting (left).

Lighting and Interior Design: Charles J. Grebmeier, ASID
Photo: Mary E. Nichols

The pendant luminaire by Boyd Lighting adds a whimsical touch to this dining room. Accent lighting is provided by recessed fixtures in the built-in hutch and a slim picture light above the art on the fireplace wall.

Lighting and Interior Design:
  Sherry Scott
Photo: John Martin

Indirect lighting above the overlapping beams shows off the crisp architectural detailing. Recessed fixtures and lighting inside the display case provide focused illumination.

Lighting and Interior Design: McDonald & Moore Ltd.
Architecture: Duncan Todd, AIA
Photo: Sharon Risedorph

A custom-crafted light sculpture floats above this residence's dining room table in Sao Paulo, Brazil.

Lighting Design: Guinter Parschalk
Interior Design and Architecture:
    Arthur de Mattos Casas
Photo: Tuca Reines

An existing art-deco-style mounting detail is enhanced by flexible low-voltage linear lighting. Dimmed to an amber glow, the lighting allows the pendant fixture over the table to stand out with its cooler color.

Lighting Design: Randall
  Whitehead, IALD, ASID
  Affiliate, and Catherine Ng, IES
Interior Design: Helen C. Reuter
Photo: Douglas A. Salin

In this residence with a distinctly Pacific Rim ambiance, subtle hidden lighting accentuates the setting, and softly colored gels add depth and mood. Indirect cove lighting crowns the table area.

Lighting and Interior Design:
Lynn Augstein, ASID, CID
  Affiliate
Photo: Douglas A. Salin

A giant Slinky-like sculpture dominates this Osaka dining room. The hollow tubing serves as a wire-way for the pendant fixture over the table.

Lighting Design:
  Kousaku Matsumoto,
  IEI Japan
Interior Design: Seiji Tanaka
Architecture: Seiji Tanaka
Photo: Yoshihisa Araki/
  Toshiya Toyoda

The depth of the cove is enhanced because the lower ceiling is silhouetted against the higher one. Light reinforces the separation and makes the upper ceiling appear to float.

Lighting Design: Steven L. Klein
Interior Design: Bill Manly, ASID
Photo: Eric Oxendorf

Cabinets illuminated from within by tiny 12-volt downlights create a sense of transparency between the dining room and hall. The table is cross-lit by two MR16 pinhole adjustable accent lights that are controlled separately from the chandelier.

Lighting Design: Steven L. Klein
Interior Design: James Mark Connelly
Architecture: Richard Sherer
Photo: Mark F. Heffron

A sculptural pendant fixture by Neidhardt artfully

adds accent light to the table.

Lighting and Interior Design: Stella Tuttle
Photo: Russell Abraham

The luminaire over the dining table provides accent

lighting and brings a strong sculptural element to the

room. Recessed adjustable downlights create additional

highlighting.

Lighting Design: Becca Foster, IES, DLF
Photo: Sharon Risedorph

Miniature low-voltage track heads mounted on the

beams' undersides provide accent lighting. Candles in

the wrought-iron wall sconce add a decorative touch.

Lighting and Interior Design: Donald Maxcy, ASID
Photo: Russell Abraham

Shoji screens separate the dining room from other

areas without blocking light. Backlighted bamboo

creates a silhouette pattern on the delicate rice paper.

The hallway leading to the dining room (left) stands

out due to indirect lighting below the skylight detail.

Lighting Design: Linda Ferry, IES, ASID Affiliate
Interior Design: John Schneider
Architecture: William David Martin, AIA
Photo: Douglas A. Salin

A floating ceiling soffit provides both accent lighting for the table and ambient lighting for the room. By keeping the illumination close to the ceiling, the view remains unobstructed.

Lighting Design: Michael Souter, ASID
Photo: Russell Abraham

A halogen bridge system provides accent lighting for this open-plan loft space. Translucent wall sconces add fill light.

Lighting Design:
    Catherine Ng, IES, and
    Randall Whitehead, IALD,
    ASID Affiliate
Interior Design:
    Joseph Ruggiero & Assoc.
Photo: Russell Abraham

Incandescent strip lights integrated into the fascia provide a wash of light on the bookshelves, while additional strip lights integrated above the crown molding show off the ceiling's architectural details. A framing projector mounted above the crown molding highlights the painting on the wall.

Lighting Design: Charles K. Thompson, AIA,
    IALD, IESNA
Interior Design: Joe Prados
Architecture: Charles Southall
Photo: Paul Bardagjy

KITCHENS
TODAY'S GATHERING PLACE

The kitchen is the new center for entertaining, a preferred site for guests to congregate while the meal is being prepared. The reasons for this trend are many, from our culture's more relaxed attitudes, to the trend toward open-plan houses.

The impact on lighting is that today's kitchens should be as inviting as the rest of the house. Kitchens, too, must have controllable lighting levels, so that guests look good and feel comfortable. The color temperatures of the lamps should match, or at least be similar to, color temperatures in other areas of the house.

Sadly, many new kitchens – even very expensive ones – still are designed with only a single source of illumination in the center of the room. Whether incandescent or fluorescent, this luminaire essentially is a glare bomb that provides little in the way of adequate task, ambient, or accent

lighting. As the eye adjusts to the glare, the rest of the kitchen seems even darker than it is.

The same rule applies to lighting kitchens as other parts of the house: No single luminaire can perform all the functions of illumination at once. A layering of various light sources is essential. Many kitchen lighting solutions of past decades – the surface-mounted single luminaire, track lighting running down the ceiling center, a series of recessed downlights installed in a grid pattern – all present similar problems. They cast harsh unflattering shadows on

faces, and while performing kitchen tasks your own head eclipses the work surface. A well-thought-out lighting design, however, avoids these negatives.

Under-Cabinet Task Lighting

One key kitchen solution is lighting that is mounted below the upper cabinets which provides even illumination on the counter-tops. Since the lighting is between your head and the work surface, shadows are minimized. When planning, though, remember that placement is important. For instance, when fluorescent strip luminaires are mounted toward the back of the cabinet, the light can

hit diners sitting in the breakfast area right in the eye. A better alternative is linear incandescent or fluorescent task lights that mount toward the cabinet front. They project part of the illumination toward the backsplash, which then bounces onto the work surface and into the center of the kitchen. This works particularly well when the countertop surface is a non-specular material.

Spreading the Light

Many alternatives are available for ambient lighting. One possibility, if a kitchen has 9-foot (2.7-meter) ceilings or higher, is to install a series of opaque or translucent pendant-hung luminaires along the space's centerline. Not only will the pendants produce wonderful ambient illumination, but they also will add a more human scale to the kitchen.

Another popular option is installing fixtures above the cabinets to provide indirect lighting. Mount the fixtures flush with the cabinet front to prevent bright spots and to make sure displayed objects don't block the light. Add blocking that lifts decorative items to the fascia level, so they are not visually cut off at the bottom.

Highlighting Artwork

You might have a few art pieces that can stand up to an occasional splash of marinara sauce. Highlighting them helps make the kitchen blend into rest of the home. Once the party has moved to another area of an open-plan house, leaving on the accent lighting while dimming the kitchen's ambient and task lighting creates a tasty effect.

Recessed downlights offer task lighting at the sink area and add texture to the louvered shutters, while additional recessed adjustable fixtures focus on the art. An alabaster fixture brings fill light to the space.

Lighting and Interior Design:
    Donald Maxcy, ASID
Photo: Russell Abraham

(Overleaf) Translucent Mirano glass pendants do a terrific job of providing overall illumination for the kitchen. Recessed fixtures with black reflectors direct additional task light onto work surfaces, as do lights mounted below the upper cabinets.

Lighting Design:
    Randall Whitehead, IALD, ASID Affiliate, and
    Catherine Ng, IES
Interior Design: Toby Flax
Architecture: Teri Behm
Photo: Cesar Rubio

Low-voltage track fixtures mounted at the apex beam

cross-illuminate the island's work surface. Indirect

lighting adds fill light and enhances the architecture.

Lighting Design: Linda Ferry, IES, ASID Affiliate
Interior Design: John Newcomb
Architecture: Stephen Wilmot
Photo: Douglas A. Salin

The grid pattern above the kitchen hides adjustable

task lighting, while under-cabinet lighting provides

additional illumination for work.

Lighting Design: Linda Ferry, IES, ASID Affiliate
Architecture: David Allen Smith
Photo: Douglas A. Salin

This large, well-appointed kitchen opens into the living and family room area. Pendant fixtures help create a sense of separation between the various spaces.

Lighting and Interior Design: Catherine Ng, IES, and
    Randall Whitehead, IALD, ASID Affiliate
Interior Design: Jessica Hall & Associates
Photo: Dennis Anderson

Fill light comes from two pendant-hung indirect fixtures. Black track heads illuminate the architectural detail above the cabinets.

Lighting and Interior Design: Ace Architects
Architecture: Ace Architects
Photo: Russell Abraham

Spherical pendants provide task lighting for the center island. A combination direct and indirect pendant fixture over the table gives both fill and accent light.

Lighting Design:
    Michael Souter, IALD, ASID
Interior Design:
    Barbara Jacobs, ASID
Photo: Douglas A. Salin

Ribbed-glass pendants supply fill light along with some task lighting, and recessed downlights provide pathway light around the center island. The countertops are illuminated by under-cabinet linear halogen fixtures.

Lighting Design and Architecture: David Ludwig
Photo: Muffy Kibbey

Incandescent alabaster pendants and dimmable fluorescent-lensed downlights provide illumination for this upscale kitchen. Fixtures within the hood and below the upper cabinets offer good task lighting on the work surfaces.

Lighting Design:
    Randall Whitehead, IALD,
    ASID Affiliate,
    and Catherine Ng, IES
Interior Design: Diane Chapman
Architecture: Mark Thomas, AIA
Photo: Michael Bruk,
    Photo/Graphics

In this updated 1930s-style kitchen, under-cabinet lighting and recessed downlights with regressed glass diffusers flood the work surfaces with illumination. A deco-influenced center fixture dishes up the necessary ambient light.

Lighting Design: Randall
  Whitehead, IALD, and
  Catherine Ng, IES
Interior Design: Christian Wright
Photo: Dennis Anderson

The most dramatic aspect of this kitchen's lighting design is the marble backsplash, which is illuminated from behind. Access to the luminaires is through the pantry, located on the other side of the wall. Under-cabinet fixtures and lighting within the cook-top hood provide excellent task light.

Lighting Design: David W. Patton
Photo: John Canham

The island in this cozy kitchen in a turn-of-the-century house is sparked by low-voltage pendants. The work areas are serviced by simple downlights and color-corrected fluorescent under-cabinet task lights.

Lighting Design:
    Ruth Soforenko, ASID,
    Debbie Collins, ASID
Interior Design:
    Ruth Soforenko, ASID
Photo: Russell Abraham

Indirect lighting within the skylight provides excellent

shadow-free task light for the kitchen, while keeping

the skylight from becoming a dark hole at night.

Lighting Design: Barbara Bouyea, IALD, IES
Interior Design: Cheri Etchelecu
Architecture: Bill Booziotis and Holly Hall
Photo: Ira Montgomery

This South American kitchen uses a triangular-shape
linear fluorescent fixture to play off the geometry of
the jet-age hood.

Lighting Design: Guinter Parschalk
Interior Design: Luiz Fernando Rocco
Architecture: Luiz Fernando Rocco/
　　Vasco Andrade Lopes
Photo: Andres Otero

This kitchen's lighting (opposite and right) is fully

integrated as an architectural detail. Illumination

from clear alzak cone-aperture downlights provides

task lighting for the island and bounces off the

surface as ambient light. A concealed 24-volt light

rail above the curving soffit emphasizes the beauty of

the architectural form.

Lighting Design: Steven L. Klein, Standard Electric
　　Supply Co.
Interior Design: Joanne Sheridan, Sturgeon Interiors, Ltd.
Architecture: Richard Sherer, Lakeside Development
Photo: Mark F. Heffron

With assistance from under-cabinet fixtures, the dark counter surfaces were effectively lit from the 12-foot- (3.7-meter) high ceilings. Precise beam spreads controlled the ambient light.

Lighting Design: Linda Ferry, IES, ASID Affiliate
Interior Design: Marilyn Riding
Architecture: Ravi Varma
Photo: Douglas A. Salin

This rich-looking kitchen with dark surfaces uses custom-designed mini-pendant luminaires to provide overall illumination.

Lighting and Interior Design: Joan Malter Osburn
Photo: Tom Wyatt

A series of individually mounted track heads adds accent light. Linear lighting mounted below the plate rack brings task illumination to the sink area.

Lighting/Interior Design: John Schneider
Kitchen Design: Sheron Bailey
Photo: Douglas A. Salin

Translucent pendant fixtures provide good work light at the island, and recessed downlights accent the china and provide pathway light.

Lighting Design: Axiom, Inc.
Interior Design: Lorraine Lazowick
Photo: Kenneth Rice

Low-voltage pendant lights provide illumination for the center island. Task lighting for the sink counter comes through generously sized windows during the daytime and from a series of recessed downlights at night.

Lighting/Interior Design and Architecture: Alan Ohashi
Photo: Russell Abraham

This kitchen's several layers of lighting are independently controlled by dimmers. Indirect 15,000-hour 5-watt xenon cove lighting above the kitchen cabinets highlights knickknacks and reflects off the ceiling. Decorative incandescent luminaires reflect off the ceiling, evening out illumination from recessed fixtures and directing light onto the granite countertops.

Lighting Design:
    Janis Huston, IES, IALD
Interior Design: Deidre Mellan
Photo: Gary Otte

Pendant fixtures provide light for the center island and work peninsula, and sleekly styled under-cabinet fixtures offer good task lighting for the countertops.

Lighting Design: Cynthia Bolton Karasik
Architecture: Joe Esherick
Photo: Russell Abraham

Recessed low-voltage fixtures light the art and tabletop, while recessed fluorescents with white diffusing lenses spread out even lighting.

Lighting Design and Architecture:
    Mark Thomas, AIA
Interior Design: Frederick Miley
Photo: Michael Bruk

Low-voltage lamps provide strong task lighting where

chores are done, and the dome-shaped fluorescent

skylight takes care of the ambient illumination.

Lighting/Interior Design and Architecture:
    David Hale, AIA
Photo: Alan Weintraub

BEDROOMS
A QUIET RETREAT

Often bedrooms are considered unimportant areas when lighting plans are put together. As a result, each bedroom gets stuck with a light in the center of the ceiling and a couple of bedside reading lamps.

But think about how much of the time we live in our bedrooms. We spend one-third of our lives sleeping, and countless more hours in the bedroom before and after sleep. When a bedroom is shared with a significant other, flattering light is particularly essential. After all, it's important to look your best in such an intimate setting.

Indirect Lighting

People are the main event in a bedroom setting. Help erase dark circles and soften age lines by providing adequate ambient light. Your partner will love you for it. If an existing luminaire is centered on the ceiling, an easy upgrade is to replace it with a pendant-hung

indirect light. This will provide illumination that bounces off the ceiling and walls to create shadow-free light. In houses with sloped ceilings, remember that the tall wall area above the door line doesn't have to be dead space. Mounting a series of two or three wall sconces there will create great fill light and not waste any art display wall space at normal viewing heights.

Cove lighting and other architectural solutions for creating ambient illumination often work beautifully in bedrooms. But if you're not ready to go that far, a pair of reasonably priced torchieres

will do the trick of throwing light on the ceiling. Also, you can place an indirect light source on top of a tall piece of furniture such as an armoire. A canopy bed with a solid top is another great location for hiding an indirect light.

Reading in Bed

In addition to ambient light, another function of illumination should be considered: task lighting for reading. If you choose the typical approach – portable luminaires (table lamps) on bedside tables – select shades with opaque liners. The liners will direct light down and across your reading matter, and also help keep the light from disturbing your bed mate.

Uplighting within the canopy emphasizes the bed,

which is the room's focal point.

Lighting Design: Donald Maxcy, ASID
Interior Design: Bill Reno
Photo: Russell Abraham

Another possibility is installing wall-mounted swing-arm lamps, a flexible source of illumination that doesn't take up bedside table space. Mounting swing-arm lamps at the correct height is critical, however. To find the ideal height, get into bed and hunker down against the pillows in your normal reading position. Then measure from the floor to just above shoulder height. Why? Because the optimum spot to position task lighting is between the head and work surface. When loved ones sharing a bed nest in at different heights, compromises should be made on both sides so the reading lights can be mounted at matching heights.

(Overleaf) This table lamp is sophisticated but whimsical, combining great texture with simple geometry.

Lighting and Interior Design: April Sheldon, CID
Photo: John Casado

A recefrom *A recessed dome is uplighted using bendable linear low-voltage luminaires, giving the room a gentle overall glow.*

Lighting Design: Axiom Design Inc.
Interior Design: Deborah Raye
Photo: Kenneth Rice

Two recessed adjustable fixtures above the bed provide reading light, similar to the individual overhead lights on airplanes.

Lighting and Interior Design: Donald Maxcy, ASID
Photo: Russell Abraham

The corner of this bedroom layers fill lighting from a single torchiere with accent lighting from recessed downlights over the window seat and in the bookcase.

Lighting and Interior Design: Donald Maxcy, ASID
Photo: Russell Abraham

Swing-arm lamps with opaque metal shades offer excellent reading light without glare.

Lighting and Interior Design:
Donald Maxcy, ASID
Photo: Russell Abraham

The sandblasted wall sconces and pendant by Johnson Art Studios lend a golden glow of illumination to this master bedroom in Sonoma, California.

Lighting Design: Randall Whitehead, IALD, ASID
    Affiliate, Catherine Ng, IES
Interior Design: Carol Saal
Architecture: Stan Field
Photo: Dennis Anderson

Beehive wall sconces by Phoenix Day Company flood light into this cool green sanctuary. A backlighted shoji panel provides a glimpse of the bonsai tree beyond, while recessed downlights show off the Chinese ceramics.

Lighting Design: Randall Whitehead, IALD, ASID
    Affiliate, and Catherine Ng, IES
Interior Design: Randall Whitehead
Photo: Dennis Anderson

A center opaque plaster pendant offers flattering ambient light, while dimmable bedside lamps provide illumination for reading.

Lighting Design: Randall Whitehead, IALD, ASID
    Affiliate, and Catherine Ng, IES
Interior Design: Christian Wright
Photo: Dennis Anderson

Inspired by a walk in the Tuileries in Paris, this flower lamp designed by April Sheldon has a base derived from some of the garden's architectural elements.

Lighting Design: April SHeldon, CID
Photo: John Casado

A row of miniature recessed downlights mounted within a soffit detail washes the wood paneling on the fireplace wall. A standing lamp with an opaque shade provides reading light without overpowering the space.

Lighting Design: Barbara Bouyea, IALD, IES
Interior Design and Architecture: Mil Bodron
Photo: Ira Montgomery

The intricately painted wall panels are evenly

illuminated with a row of recessed wall-wash fixtures

(opposite). Accent lights bring out the many gilded

items in the room. Low-voltage recessed adjustable

fixtures with black trims fade into the black ceiling

(below), allowing elements of the room to be the

primary focus.

Lighting Design: Craig Roeder, IALD
Interior Design: Loyd Ray Taylor and
   Charles Paxton Gremillion
Architecture: Hendricks & Wall
Photo: Robert Ames Cook

A lavender table lamp adds a luminous glow to

the seating area in this master bedroom suite.

The television in the console at the end of the bed

can easily be lowered when not in use.

Lighting and Interior Design: Kathy Monteiro
Photo: Doug Johnson

A deep soffit detail houses both accent and indirect lighting in this spacious master bedroom.

Lighting Design: Craig Roeder, IALD
Interior Design: Duffala/von Thaden Assoc., Inc.
Architecture: Fleischman/Garcia Architects
Photo: Jeff Blankton

Wall sconces flank the bed in this child's room. A table lamp with a perforated metal shade offers reading light without glare.

Lighting Design: Catherine Ng, IES, and
    Randall Whitehead, IALD, ASID Affiliate
Interior Design: Joseph Ruggiero & Assoc.
Photo: Russell Abraham

BATHROOMS
THE GREAT ESCAPE

Well-designed lighting is of the utmost importance in the bathroom, where the activities of grooming and self-care require excellent task lighting. Yet more often than not, homeowners and professionals install fixtures that provide inadequate illumination for tasks at the vanity and other key areas.

Remember when, as a child, you would hold a flashlight under your chin to create a scary face? The same thing happens, only in reverse, when you stand at a vanity directly under a recessed downlight or a single luminaire surface-mounted above the mirror.

Satisfying Vanity at the Vanity

For the most ideal task lighting at a vanity, set up a system of cross-illumination on the vertical axis. This can be accomplished simply by flanking the mirror with two luminaires.

The principle of cross-illumination on the vertical axis originated in the theater, where mirrors were surrounded by bare bulbs. Now homes everywhere have the residential equivalent, multi-bulb brass or chrome light bars. Remember, though, that these bars work best when mounted on either side of the mirror. A third luminaire can be mounted above the mirror, but is not necessary. Light bars aren't your only option: A more recent trend for providing cross-illumination is wall-mounting translucent luminaires at eye level on either side of the sink. Many builders and architects install fluorescent or incandescent light soffits, fitted with either acrylic diffusers or egg-crate louvers, over vanity areas. These fixtures, too, mostly illuminate the top half of a person's face, although some cross-lighting occurs from top to bottom if the light reflects off of a white or glossy counter. While not the optimum solution, this is a passable substitute if vertical cross-illumination is impossible to install.

While the vanity is the most critical spot to illuminate correctly, tubs, showers, and other areas also need good general light. For this purpose, the commonly used

recessed luminaires with white opal diffusers are relatively effective.

Fluorescents in the Bathroom

The fluorescent option is important today. Several states require fluorescent light sources in the design, construction, or remodeling of residential bathrooms, because fluorescents are at least three times more energy efficient than incandescent bulbs.

Fortunately, the color temperature of many of today's fluorescent lamps, including the newer compact fluorescent lamps (CFLs), have color-correcting phosphors that are very flattering to skin tones. Compact fluorescent lamps not only offer greatly improved color rendering, but the 13-watt version, for example, produces

illumination similar to that produced by a 60-watt incandescent bulb. Two drawbacks to some of the cheaper compact fluorescent lamps are an inherent hum and the lack of a rapid-start ballast, the latter deficiency causing the lamp to flicker two or three times before stabilizing. Some quad versions are much quieter and have a relatively rapid start-up. These advances, along with long life and dimming capability, make fluorescent lighting worth a second look.

That Special Overall Glow

Indirect lighting in a bathroom adds overall warmth and illumination, even more necessary now that bathrooms are becoming multifunctional spaces. Wall sconces or cove lighting that directs light upward can provide this

gentle ambient illumination. Both options can use miniature incandescent lamps, compact fluorescents, or standard-length fluorescent tubes. For bathrooms with higher ceilings, pendant-hung units also can be considered for fill light.

Safety First

The necessity of protecting yourself and your loved ones from electric shock demands special planning when lighting bathrooms. First, make sure that all luminaires located close to water are installed with an instant circuit shutoff, called a ground fault interrupter (GFI). In addition, select only those lighting fixtures that are listed for damp locations by the Underwriters' Laboratory (UL) or another approved testing laboratory. Products tested by the UL have a special blue label.

(Overleaf) Victorian-style wall sconces provide fill lighting for this bathroom, with additional ambient illumination coming from indirect color-corrected fluorescent cove lighting.

Lighting Design and Architecture: Richard Perlstein, AIA
Photo: Muffy Kibbey

All of the light fixtures in this bathroom are fluorescent, now a versatile and energy-efficient alternative to standard incandescent lighting. Of special note, the television is mounted behind the mirror and appears only when turned on.

Lighting Design: Michael Souter, IALD, ASID
Interior Design: Bob Miller
Photo: Douglas Salin

In this tight space, sandblasted blown-glass wall

sconces are mounted on the return walls to provide

task lighting at the mirror.

Lighting Design: Randall Whitehead, IALD, ASID
    Affiliate, and Catherine Ng, IES
Interior Design: Helen C. Reuter
Photo: Douglas A. Salin

Compact Murano glass luminaries manufactured by

Zelco were installed flush with the mirror surface,

their housings recessed into the wall before the mirror

installation. The mirror reflects a row of three

additional matching luminaries on the opposite wall.

The fixtures use a 7-watt compact fluorescent lamp.

Lighting Design: Catherine Ng, IES, and
    Randall Whitehead, IALD, ASID Affiliate
Interior Design: Lawrence Masnada
Architecture: Sid Del Mar Leach
Photo: Kenneth Rice

Lighting hidden behind a valence dramatizes the window treatments, and recessed eyeball fixtures offer reading light for long, relaxing baths.

Lighting and Interior Design: J. Hettinger Interiors
Photo: Doug Johnson

e design elements of this wild powder room work ether, with the pendant fixture by Christina Spann lected in the sheet of glass covering the wall mural. e pendant provides shadow-free fill light.

ghting and Interior Design: Lou Ann Bauer
oto: Douglas A. Salin

Pendant fixtures hover like flying saucers alongside the two mirrors in this crisply appointed bath. Daylight floods in through the glass-block wall.

Lighting Design and Architecture: Dan Frederick
Photo: Russell Abraham

A dome detail above the whirlpool sparkles with fiber-optic stars, while recessed downlights along the perimeter give off light reminiscent of comets hurtling toward the heavens.

Lighting Design: Axiom, Inc.
Interior Design: Jim Wallen and Albert Carey
Photo: David Livingston

An indirect linear low-voltage system brings out the luster of the bathroom's gold-leaf ceiling. Recessed downlights illuminate the countertops and flooring by Benattar.

Lighting Design: Axiom, Inc.
Interior Design: Jim Wallen and Albert Carey
Photo: David Livingston

Translucent wall sconces float on the mirrors above the

vanity sinks. Fill light comes from the vaulted

skylight, which has luminaires mounted within.

Lighting Design: Jared Polsky and Associates
Architecture: Jared Polsky and Associates
Photo: Jay Graham

A blend of natural and artificial light brightens up this

master bath. Tall windows provide light during the

day, with translucent halogen sconces emitting both

task and ambient illumination at night.

Lighting Design: Randall Whitehead, IALD, and
    Catherine Ng, IES
Architecture: Richard Perlstein, AIA
Photo: Muffy Kibbey

Unobtrusive recessed downlights highlight the architectural elements and varied textures.

Lighting/Interior Design and
    Architecture: Charles J.
    Grebmeier, ASID, Grebmeier-
Roy Design
Photo: Eric Zepeda

Pendants in the Arts and Crafts style address the need for task lighting at the vanity (right). The tub is bathed in soft light from fixtures on wall brackets (above). The light well is uplighted to offer additional fill illumination at night.

Lighting Design and Architecture: David Ludwig
Photo: Muffy Kibbey

The designer selected Robbia sconces by Ve Art to
provide even cross-illumination at the mirror. A row of
miniature recessed downlights washes a wall visible in
the mirror's reflection.

Lighting Design: Barbara Bouyea, IALD, IES
Interior Design: Cheri Etchelecu
Architecture: Bill Booziotis and Holly Hall
Photo: Ira Montgomery

Blown-glass sconces mounted on the mirror provide
even illumination for tasks at the sink. The translucent
glass basin glows from luminaires installed below
the counter.

Lighting Design: Barbara Bouyea, IALD, IES.
Interior Design and Architecture: Mil Bodron
Photo: Ira Montgomery

Clerestory windows bring precious natural light into this bathroom, with halogen wall sconces providing illumination at night. A makeup mirror with integrated lighting gives good, shadow-free task illumination.

Lighting Design and Architecture: David Ludwig
Photo: Muffy Kibbey

The slot opening between the wall and ceiling is the perfect place for concealing the warm fluorescent light source that gives the tub area a golden glow.

Lighting Design: Barbara Bouyea, IALD, IES
Interior Design: Allen Kirsch
Photo: Ira Montgomery

The luminaire on the mirror was specially designed to provide a light level that is soft yet sufficiently bright for performing tasks, while also minimizing glare from bulbs.

Lighting Design: Guinter Parschalk
Architecture: Candida Tabet
Photo: Tuca Reines

Rather than installing decorative lighting fixtures in this master bath, downlights with prismatic glass lenses were used to create a bright, even field of light at the mirror.

Lighting Design: Bradley A. Bouch
Interior Design: Jacqueline Thornton
Architecture: Richard Luke
Photo: Dave Chawla

Lighting mounted beneath the cabinets creates a wonderful night light, while Italian glass fixtures provide good task light at the sink.

Lighting and Interior Design:
   Joan Malter Osburn
Photo: Philip Harvey

Translucent glass and metal fixtures use halogen sources to provide fill light. Recessed fixtures with frosted glass trims offer additional illumination.

Lighting Design: Becca Foster
    IES, DLF
Photo: Sharon Risedorph

The small luminous glass tiles

in the floor are backlighted with

fiber optics.

Lighting and Interior Design:
    Joan Malter Osburn
Photo: Philip Harvey

The design challenge was to

provide a mirror and lighting

for the sink that allowed the

window to remain unblocked.

Lighting and Interior Design:
    April Sheldon, CID
Photo: John Casado

The illuminated scalloped glass

canopy over the mirror is a

modern-day interpretation of

French architecture.

Lighting and Interior Design:
    Joan Malter Osburn
Photo: John Vaughan

SPECIALTY AREAS
BREAKING THROUGH THE BOUNDARIES

The spaces found in this chapter range from beautifully done transitional areas such as hallways and stairs, to very functional areas such as home offices and rooms for watching television, to more esoteric areas such as wine cellars and a fantasy playroom for children.

Home Offices

People are simply living differently than previous generations. Retirees are starting second careers out of their homes, while the younger generation is making the leap to home offices as part of preparing for life in the next millennium. How do you make this office space usable and comfortable? If the office area is visible from the rest of the house, how do you blend the work-oriented space with the overall look of the home? The answer lies with the appropriate use of color, texture, round edges, plush carpeting, plants, and comfortably layered illumination.

A common misconception is the more light there is, the better people can see. In the case of computer monitors if there is too much light in the room, the screen becomes difficult to read. Another factor is the difference in brightness between what the person is working on at their desk, and the screen itself. Going back and forth from a brightly illuminated document to a more dimly lit screen will cause eye fatigue. Bouncing a soft wash of illumination off the ceiling will lessen the contrast.

Layered with this general illumination should be some flexible task-oriented lighting. A tabletop or wall-mounted luminaire with a flexible arm and variability in light levels is a good way of lighting documents and keyboard without spilling light onto the screen itself. Select a fixture with an opaque shade so the image of the luminaire itself won't reflect onto the monitor.

Home Entertainment

Not only are people working out of the house, they are also bringing entertainment home. The home theater industry is booming and the traditional living room is reflecting the change. These rooms can be exclusively designed for the entertaining factor, or incorporated into multi-use spaces that double

This gallery-inspired passageway takes full advantage of the high ceiling. Concealed light sources bring out the strong architectural detailing, while recessed fixtures show off the collection of art.

Lighting Design: Linda Ferry, IES, ASID Affiliate
Architecture: David Allen Smith
Photo: Douglas A. Salin

(Overleaf) Lighting under the nosing of the steps makes this spiral staircase look like a glowing nautilus shell.

Lighting Design: Craig Roeder, IALD
Interior Design: Loyd Ray Taylor and
    Charles Paxton Gremillion
Architecture: Hendricks & Wall
Photo: Robert Ames Cook

as guest rooms with beds hidden in walls or surprisingly comfortable sofas.

These rooms need a variety of light levels to adapt to the different uses. A theater setting would have the light dimmed to a slight glow with a small amount of path lighting in order to move in and out of the room safely. The guest room would need a good deal of ambient light with some bedside task lighting in order to be comfortable and accommodating.

Transitional Areas

Although these areas are often referred to as throwaway spaces, hallways, stairs, and landings can be transformed into areas of interest with the use of color, art, plants, and lighting. Think of them as display areas, vignettes that show off your prized possessions or collections. Well-lit hallways and stairs can entice guests through your home and give hints of the enchanting spaces to come. The lighting here can be highly dramatic, lending texture and dimension to often overlooked spaces.

Luminaires with dichroic filters make a dramatic

proscenium for this rear-screen-projection home

theater. A halogen bridge system spotlights the orchid,

while a black-shaded lamp lights the table behind the

sofa without reflecting on the screen.

Lighting and Interior Design: Michael Souter, IALD,
    ASID
Photo: Douglas A. Salin

Two direct/indirect pendant fixtures give this library room an overall glow while also providing light for the desk surface. Recessed fixtures and picture lights accent the carvings and other art pieces.

Lighting Design: Michael Souter, IALD, ASID
Interior Design: Rhonda Luongo, ASID, CCID
Architecture: Albert Pastine
Photo: Douglas A. Salin

This dressing room benefits from the bright glow of fluorescent fixtures mounted behind a flowing run of cloth and braided rope.

Lighting Design: Axiom Design Inc.
Interior Design: Tina Messner
Photo: Kenneth Rice

This transitional space gives the art a tremendous amount of breathing room. Recessed adjustable fixtures highlight the pieces, with wall sconces providing the overall illumination.

Lighting Design:
    Michael Souter, IALD, ASID
Interior Design:
    Rhonda Luongo, ASID, CCID
Architecture: Albert Pastine
Photo: Douglas A. Salin

A group of wall sconces on dimmers adds a flexible amount of ambient lighting to this home theater. A framing projector cuts a precise rectangle of illumination for the center painting.

Lighting and Interior Design: J. Hettinger Interiors
Photo: Doug Johnson

Recessed adjustable fixtures cross-illuminate the desktop in this home office. Shelf-mounted linear incandescent task lights provide illumination along the back work surface.

Lighting and Interior Design:
  J. Hettinger Interiors
Photo: Doug Johnson

The Art of Lighting

Exposed blue-green neon contrasts with indirect

red neon to help illuminate this dynamic

multifunctional space.

Lighting and Interior Design: Donald Maxcy, ASID
Photo: Russell Abraham

This incredible fantasy room designed for the homeowner's children combines elements of a Mayan temple, disco, and video arcade. The view from the balcony (opposite) shows palm trees illuminated by recessed fixtures and wall sconces that hint at an earlier civilization. The rotating mirror ball (right) creates an ever-moving star pattern on the walls and ceiling.

Lighting and Interior Design:
    Donald Maxcy, ASID
Photo: Russell Abraham

The hallway to the bedrooms becomes a background for projected light patterns of stripes and stars. Recessed framing projectors are fitted with custom templates to create the shapes of light.

Lighting Design: Craig Roeder, IALD
Interior Design: Loyd Ray Taylor and
    Charles Paxton Gremillion
Photo: Robert Ames Cook

Recessed adjustable fixtures show off the art, a crown molding detail hides a run of low-voltage perimeter lighting, and a center luminaire by Johnson Art Studios introduces additional fill light.

Lighting Design: Randall Whitehead, IALD,
    and Catherine Ng, IES
Interior Design: Courtney Griffith
Photo: Dennis Anderson

In this home theater, black track fixtures disappear against the black ceiling and give the burgundy velvet curtain a rich luster. A perimeter run of low-voltage tube lighting adds a theatrical touch.

Lighting/Interior Design and Architecture:
    Roeder Johnson
Photo: Russell Abraham

In this striking theater, indirect low-voltage lighting creates a corona of illumination along the inset ceiling detail. Additional recessed fixtures light up the niches and center ottomans, and translucent wall sconces add warm sparkle.

Lighting Design: Duane Johnson, IESNA
Photo: John Sutton

This lighting system creates a gallery-like display while also providing general lighting.

Lighting Design: Bradley A. Bouch
Interior Design: Jacqueline Thornton
Architecture: Richard Luke
Photo: Dave Chawla

A lavender filter turns this wet bar into a mesmerizing blend of hot and cold colors.

Lighting Design: Craig Roeder, IALD
Interior Design: Loyd Ray Taylor and Charles Paxton
  Gremillion
Architecture: Hendricks & Wall
Photo: Robert Ames Cook

In this beautiful wine cellar, a single light source shows off the selection of wines being offered for tasting. Indirect lighting enhances the barrel-vault ceiling, while individual shelf lighting illuminates other vintages in the collection.

Lighting Design: Duane Johnson,
     IESNA
Interior Design: Cathy Wentz
Architecture: Ron Sutton, AIA
Photo: John Sutton

Low-profile recessed adjustable fixtures add drama to this transitional space. A very architectural indirect luminaire can be seen in the dining area beyond, where it provides ambient illumination.

Lighting Design: Barbara Bouyea, IALD, IES
Interior Design: Cheri Etchelecu
Architecture: Bill Booziotis and Holly Hall
Photo: Ira Montgomery

The light fixture was custom designed for the client's wonderful curved hallway to illuminate the artwork and make its own design statement. The fixture has a brass and pewter finish and uses line-voltage lamps.

Lighting Design: Terry Ohm
Interior Design: Anne Maurice
Photo: Robert Bengtson

Under-cabinet lights and a table lamp provide the recessing task light in this home office.

Lighting and Interior Design: Sandra Brown
Photo: Doug Johnson

This cleanly designed home theater benefits from cov lighting which, along with recessed-aperture downlights, provides illumination without reflecting onto the screen.

Lighting Design: Randall Whitehead, IALD, ASID
    Affiliate, Catherine Ng, IES
Interior Design: Casey Grenier
Architecture: Anthony Ngai
Photo: Dennis Anderson

Exterior Spaces
BRINGING THE OUTDOORS INSIDE

When thinking about lighting for your home, you may not see a need to incorporate exterior lighting into the overall design. In reality, though, the illumination of exterior spaces has a direct impact on how people perceive interior areas.

Exterior lighting visually expands the interior rooms of a residence. When there is no illumination outside, the black-mirror effect occurs: Windows reflect interior lights, making people feel boxed in and the space seem smaller. When they can see the yard, guests feel safer and no longer on display. Balancing the amount of light inside and outside the house allows the windows to become more transparent.

Now don't think you have to light up the exterior like the White House. That type of illumination comes under the heading of security lighting, which is very different from landscape lighting.

Yet people often will try to use the same lights to perform both functions. Security lighting usually is a source of blasting light which, when switched on, immediately floods a yard. Landscape lighting, on the other hand, needs to be subtle. Attention should be drawn to the plantings, sculpture, and outbuildings, not to the lighting itself.

Decorative exterior luminaires such as lanterns can't do the job by themselves without becoming disturbing hot spots that leave everything else in silhouette. Still, they serve the same important purpose as interior decorative

luminaires. An exterior lantern creates the illusion of providing all the landscape lighting, when, in reality, it may put out no more than 25 watts of illumination.

Landscape Lighting Techniques

Choose several options from the wide variety of landscape illumination techniques, since layering adds visual interest to exterior lighting.

Uplighting This can be a very dramatic way to light trees that have a sculptural quality. The luminaires can be ground-mounted or installed below grade. These buried luminaires, known as well lights, have little or no adjustability,

Cool-colored light sources mounted along the deck's underside bring out the silvery-blue tones of the moss-covered branches. The flames of large-scale votive candles make for a warm contrast.

Lighting Design: Randall Whitehead, IALD, ASID
    Affiliate, and Catherine Ng, IES
Architecture: David Gast
Photo: Kenneth Rice

(Overleaf) Recessed downlights mounted in the overhangs cast pools of light along the perimeter of the house. A blue filter on the pool light keeps the water from looking too yellow.

Lighting and Architecture: Gordon Stein
Photo: Douglas A. Salin

so they aren't the best choice for rapidly growing trees. Above-ground directional luminaires, which shrubbery easily can conceal, have much greater flexibility.

Silhouetting Particularly in the winter, deciduous trees often look better when left dark with the wall behind them illuminated. Many fluorescent luminaires can do a good job of wall-washing for a small amount of power and long lamp life. Remember to specify a ballast designed for low temperatures if you live in a cold region.

Downlighting Good for outdoor activity areas, downlighting luminaires can be mounted on trellises, eaves, gazebos, and mature trees. To reduce shadowing, overlap the luminaires' spreads of illumination.

Path Lighting Use this lighting technique judiciously. Too often, pagoda-type path lights are the only source of exterior illumination, causing walkways or driveways to look like an airport runway. When a pathway light is needed, consider using an opaque mushroom-type luminaire that projects light downward without drawing attention to itself.

Moonlighting By mounting luminaires relatively high in mature trees, a dappled pattern of light and shadow is created on pathways and low-level plantings. Moonlighting, as this is called, looks very natural.

Light sources with a variety of color temperatures help

create this fantasy-like setting, with adjustable

ground-mounted fixtures highlighting trunks and

branches. Here, a sprinkling of rain turns the

driveway into a temporary reflecting pool.

Lighting Design: Randall Whitehead, IALD, ASID
    Affiliate, and Catherine Ng, IES
Architecture: David Gast
Photo: Kenneth Rice

This quiet water feature is beautifully illuminated by discreetly placed luminaires. Miniature low-voltage fixtures are tucked in between the rocks to uplight the trees, while additional units mounted in the overhanging branches throw shadows onto the rocks.

Lighting Design: Linda Ferry, IES, ASID Affiliate
Architecture: David Allen Smith
Photo: Douglas A. Salin

Viewed from the house, the illuminated oak trees become huge sculptural elements. To add dimension and depth, the miniature low-voltage luminaires mounted within the trees use various hues of blue. Fixtures mounted below the deck uplight the canopy of foliage.

Lighting Design:
   Randall Whitehead, IALD, ASID Affiliate,
   and Catherine Ng, IES
Architecture: David Gast
Photo: Kenneth Rice

This front entry is located in an enclosed courtyard. Recessed downlights by Capri highlight the doorway and the window niches.

Lighting Design:
   Linda Ferry, IES, ASID Affiliate
Architecture: Lee von Hasseln
Photo: Douglas A. Salin

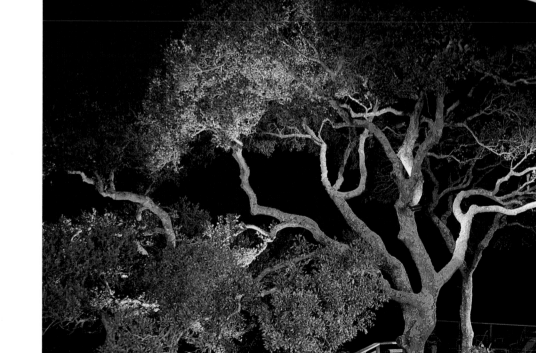

Individual uplights highlight the miniature citrus trees, while an additional uplight illuminates the large trunk. Luminaires mounted in the tree's branches offer path lighting.

Lighting Design: Anna Victoria Kondolf
Landscape Design: Stephen Suzman
Photo: Douglas A. Salin

Subtly illuminated archways frame the garden area beyond, where an individual spotlights focuses on each of the bromeliads in the center tree. Downlighting from the right gives volume to the canopy of foliage.

Lighting Design: Anna Victoria Kondolf
Landscape Design: Stephen Suzman
Photo: Douglas A. Salin

Moonlight from behind the trees creates a dappled pattern of light and shadow across the rockscape. Blue filters keep the water looking cool and fresh.

Lighting and Pool Design: Russel Greey
Photo: Douglas A. Salin

In keeping with the tropical setting, tiki torches

surrounding these island homes send out a warm-

spirited welcome.

Lighting Design and Architecture: Lucky Bennett
Photo: Russell Abraham

The Art of Lighting

Luminaires mounted on the columns and exterior walls add a glimmer of light without overpowering the environment. Fixtures installed between the beams add pathway lighting for this home in Japan.

Lighting Design:
   Kousaku Matsumoto,
   IEI Japan
Architecture: Seiji Tanaka
Photo: Yoshihisa Araki/
   Toshiya Toyoda

The pool lights are fitted with blue fixtures to turn the water a dramatic azure color (opposite). Lighting inside and outside the house transforms it into a luminous sculpture. The living room (right) forms a bridge above the swimming pool. Indirect lighting keeps the windows free of reflections.

Lighting Design: Guinter Parschalk,
    RDX-Radix Commercial LTD.
Interior Design: Luiz Fernando Rocco
Architecture: Luiz Fernando Rocco/
    Vasco Andrade Lopes
Photo: Andres Otero

This home on the California coast glows brightly at night. Ambient light fills the interior space, while downlights tucked under the eaves illuminate the deck.

Lighting and Interior Design: Don Maxcy, ASID
Photo: Russell Abraham

LIGHTING Q AND A

ANSWERS TO FREQUENTLY ASKED LIGHTING QUESTIONS

As a lighting consultant and lecturer with many years of experience, I find that the homeowners, architects, interior designers, and landscape architects with whom I work often raise similar questions. Some of their concerns relate to basics about lighting design. Other questions come up because more and more new products constantly are appearing on the market, and consumers easily can become confused while trying to keep abreast of the latest technology. The field is indeed changing rapidly, and learning about lighting is an ongoing process.

What are the main things to consider when selecting lighting for residential use?

First, assess the amount of light needed for a given space. This is determined by functional needs, the height and slope of the ceiling, the color of the room's surfaces, the location of windows and skylights, and the direction the house faces. Second, consider the proper type of lamps (bulbs) to use for good color rendering of the various surfaces in the space. Try to keep the color temperature of the lamps between 3,000 and 4,000 degrees Kelvin, no matter what source. You can mix incandescent, halogen, fluorescent, low-voltage, and line-voltage sources, as long as their color temperatures are similar.

What are the recommended mounting heights for wall sconces and ceiling fixtures?

Wall sconces normally are mounted at 6 feet (1.8 meters) on 8-foot (2.4-meter) walls and at 6.6 feet (2 meters) on walls that are 9 feet (2.7 meters) or taller. A pendant-hung fixture normally is mounted 36 inches (91 centimeters) above the table or countertop.

Should I install track or recessed lighting?

Track lighting works best when used as accent lighting to highlight paintings and specific objects, and it's a particularly good option when there is not enough ceiling depth for recessed lighting, or in rental units where cost and portability are important. Track lighting does not, however, provide adequate ambient light to warm and soften a room. It also is a poor choice for task lighting, because you end up working in your own shadow.

Over the past several years, recessed lighting has greatly improved. Most manufacturers now offer recessed adjustable fixtures that use low-voltage lamps

(lamp is the lighting industry's term for a light bulb) and integral transformers. These fixtures offer the clean look of a recessed system with the flexibility of track, and a wide variety of beam spreads can be produced simply by changing the lamp. The big news, however, is that now many of these fixtures are made specifically for remodeling, which makes installation into existing ceilings clean and easy.

What is the best way to avoid glare when lighting artwork on a wall?

Accent light fixtures, such as recessed adjustable and track, should have louvers and be directed onto art from the side, instead of centered on the painting. Any glass or Plexiglas surface becomes a mirror. If the light comes from the side, then the glare is redirected away from the viewer.

What about the energy efficiency of various lighting options?

Incandescent household bulbs are the least energy-efficient choice.

Halogen lamps supply approximately twice the amount of light provided by household bulbs of the same wattage. Fluorescents are three to five times more energy efficient than comparable incandescent household bulbs.

How can I get both the color quality of incandescent light and the energy efficiency of fluorescent?

For years, the only choices in fluorescent lamps were warm-white, which actually looked like a blend of pink and orange, and cool-white, which produced a blue-green light that made people look ghoulish. Today all that has changed, and more than 200 colors of fluorescents are available. In addition, the technology of fluorescent components has

improved to include a non-humming, full-range dimming ballast line of fixtures.

Should I consider compact fluorescent lamps (CFLs)?

Yes, particularly since this energy-efficient option now comes in such a variety of color temperatures. In addition, CFLs are available that are inside glass envelopes with standard screw-in bases, so the look of the lamps is comfortably familiar. A 9-watt CFL produces light roughly equivalent to 40 watts of incandescent illumination, while a 13-watt CFL is approximately equal to 75 watts worth of incandescent light.

What is a low-voltage lighting system, and what are its advantages?

Low voltage, according to electrical code, is anything under 50 volts (normal house current, also known as line voltage, operates at 110 to 120 volts). The most commonly used low-voltage systems are 12-volt and 6-volt. A transformer lowers line voltage to low voltage. It can be located inside the fixture (integral) or somewhere nearby (remote).Low voltage can produce more light per watt than line voltage—often at as much as a three-to-one ratio. Although low-voltage systems have a higher initial cost, the advantages in energy efficiency and low maintenance are considerable. Low-voltage lamps come in a variety of wattages and beam spreads; you can pinpoint a bowl of flowers or light a 6-foot (1.8-meter) painting. Currently the most popular low-voltage lamp is the MR16 (multi-mirror reflector), the same type of lamp used in slide projectors.

What is a halogen bulb?

Halogen, also referred to as tungsten halogen or quartz, is an incandescent source that burns at a

whiter color temperature than a standard household bulb. As a result, colors are rendered more truly in a space illuminated by halogen. However, like all incandescent sources, a halogen lamp will become more amber when dimmed. Because a halogen lamp has much greater light output than a standard household bulb of equal wattage, you can use a smaller wattage halogen lamp to give an equal amount of light. Halogen sources come in low and line voltage versions.

Can a halogen bulb be touched?

It's best not to touch the glass envelope of most halogen lamps. The oil on your hand attracts dirt to the glass and can create a point of weakness, causing the bulb to burn out prematurely and possibly explode. If you do happen to touch the lamp, clean it with rubbing alcohol.

Do halogen bulbs last longer?

The average rated life for a halogen lamp is 2,000 to 2,500 hours. This means that at the 2,000- to 2,500-hour mark, half the lamps will be burned out and half will still be working. The key to maximizing halogen lamp life is to make sure the bulb runs at full capacity (turned up all the way rather than dimmed) at least 20 percent of the time it is used. This has a cleaning effect on the inside of the lamp.

If halogen torchieres direct light upward, how can they provide light suitable for reading?

Halogen torchieres provide excellent ambient lighting for a room. If you have a white or light colored ceiling, they also can provide suitable secondary task illumination for reading. However, this reflected light should be used

only for light reading, such as perusing newspapers or magazines. For serious reading of books, the best option is a pharmacy-type lamp that positions the light between your head and the page.

For serious reading, is the equivalent of a 60-watt incandescent bulb bright *enough*?

Light levels are a matter of preference, and the distance a person sits from the light source also is a factor. In general, the incandescent bulb in a pharmacy-type lamp which is situated next to the reader at shoulder height should be between 60 and 75 watts.

What are the guidelines for installing skylights?

Often skylights are installed to supplement or replace electric lighting during the daytime hours. Because clear or bronze skylights project a hard light in the shape of the skylight itself onto the floor, select instead a white opal skylight, which diffuses the daylight. Also, always get an ultraviolet inhibitor. It's a standard option and prevents the premature fading and sun-rotting of natural materials.

Skylights usually should not be centered over tables or islands because they interfere with the placement of lighting fixtures. However, if the light well is deep enough, fluorescent strip lights can be mounted between the acrylic panel and the skylight to provide nighttime lighting and to keep the skylight from looking like a black hole in the ceiling.

What about using neon and fiber optics for residential lighting?

Local electrical codes should be checked before using neon, since some jurisdictions don't permit it in residential spaces. Humming is another consideration. Neon is fine in rooms that have a fair amount of ambient noise, but in quiet areas the inherent hum can be disturbing unless the transformer is put in a remote location. Also, be careful with color selection, since intense

neon hues can shift a room's color scheme.

Fiber optics provide a subtle glow of light for edge details, serving as a decorative source only. The illumination from a fiber-optic fixture will be even as long as the fiber optic is looped back into the light source or illuminated from both ends. Otherwise the lighting will be more intense at one end.

GLOSSARY

Absorption: The amount of light taken in by an object instead of being reflected. Dark-colored and matte surfaces have high degrees of absorption.

Accent Lighting: Illumination directed at a particular object in order to draw attention to it.

Ambient Lighting: The soft indirect illumination that fills the volume of a room and creates an inviting glow. Also referred to as fill light.

Amperage: The amount of electrical current that can run through a conductive source.

Ballast: A device that transforms electrical energy used by fluorescent, mercury vapor, high-pressure sodium, or metal halide lamps so that the proper amount of power is provided to the lamp.

Beam Spread: The diameter of the pattern of light produced by a lamp or lamp and luminaire together.

Bridge System: A two-wire low-voltage cable lighting system.

Cold Cathode: A neon-like electric-discharge light source, often a good option for areas that cannot accommodate fluorescent tubes.

Color Rendering Index (CRI): A scale used to measure how well a lamp illuminates an object's color tones as compared with daylight. Color correction refers to the addition of phosphors to a lamp to create a better CRI.

Diffusion Filter: A glass lens used to widen and soften light output.

Dimming Ballast: A device used with fluorescent lamps to control the light level.

Fiber Optic: An illuminating system composed of a lamp source, fibers, and output optics, used to remotely light an area or object.

Filter: A glass or metal accessory that alters beam patterns.

Fluorescent Lamp: A very energy-efficient lamp that produces light by activating the phosphor coating on the inside surface of a glass envelope.

Framing Projector: A luminaire that can be precisely adjusted to frame an object with light.

Glare or Glare Factor: Uncomfortably bright light that becomes the focus of attention

rather than the area or object it was meant to illuminate.

Halogen: An incandescent lamp containing halogen gas which recycles tungsten. Halogen lamps burn hotter and brighter than standard incandescent lamps.

High-Intensity Discharge (HID) Lamp: A type of lamp primarily used in exterior settings that emits bright, energy-efficient light by electrically activating pressurized gas in a bulb. Mercury vapor, metal halide, and high-pressure sodium lamps are all HID sources.

Housing: The above-the-ceiling enclosure for a luminaire's recessed socket and trim.

Incandescent Lamp: The traditional type of light bulb that produces light through electricity causing a filament to glow.

Kelvin: A measure of color temperature.

Kilowatt: A measure of electrical usage. One thousand watts equals one kilowatt.

Lamp: The lighting industry's term for a light bulb, i.e. a glass envelope with a coating, filament, or gas that glows when electricity is applied.

Line Voltage: The 120-volt household current generally standard in North America.

Louver: A metal accessory used on a luminaire to prevent glare.

Low-Pressure Sodium Lamp: A discharge lamp that uses sodium vapor as the light-producing element. It produces an orange-gray light.

Low-Voltage Lighting: A system that uses a current less than 50 volts (commonly 12 volts)

instead of the standard household current of 120 volts. A transformer converts the electrical power to the appropriate voltage.

Luminaire: The complete light fixture with all parts and lamps (bulbs) necessary for positioning and obtaining power supply.

Mirror Reflector Lamps (i.e. MR11, MR16): Miniature tungsten halogen lamps with a variety of wattages and beam spreads, controlled by mirrors positioned in the reflector.

Neon Light: A glass vacuum tube filled with neon gas and phosphors, frequently formed into signs or letters.

PAR Lamps: Lamps (bulbs) with parabolic aluminized reflectors that give exacting beam control ranging from a wide flood to a very narrow spot. PAR lamps can be used outdoors due to their thick glass, which holds up in severe weather conditions.

R Lamp: An incandescent source with a built-in reflecting surface.

Reflectance: The ratio of light reflected from a surface.

Reflected Ceiling Plan: A lighting plan drawn from the floor looking at the ceiling above.

RLM Reflector: A luminaire designed to reflect light down, preventing upward transmission.

Spread Lens: A glass lenses accessory used to diffuse and widen beam patterns.

Task Lighting: Illumination designed for a work surface so that good light, free of shadows and glare, is present.

Transformer: A device that raises or lowers voltage, generally used for low-voltage lights.

Voltage: A measurement of the pressure of electricity going through a wire.

Voltage Drop: A decrease of electrical pressure in a low-voltage lighting system which occurs as a fixture's distance from the transformer increases, causing a drop in the light output.

White Light: Usually refers to light with a color temperature between 5,000 and 6,250 degrees Kelvin which is composed of the entire visible light spectrum. This light allows all colors in the spectrum on an object's surface to be reflected, providing good color-rendering qualities. Daylight is the most common source of white light.

Xenon: An inert gas used as a component in certain lamps to produce a cooler color temperature than standard incandescent. Xenon results in a longer lamp life than halogen.

DIRECTORY

Architects

Ace Architects
330 2nd Street, Suite 1
Oakland, CA 94607
Phone: 510-452-0775
Fax: 510-452-1175

Richard Bartlett, AIA
Theatre Square, Suite 217
Orinda, CA 94563
Phone: 510-253-2880
Fax: 510-253-2881

Teri Behm
Behm Architects
1325 Filbert Street
San Francisco, CA 94109
Phone: 415-263-1755
Fax: 415-263-1759

Hamlet C. "Lucky" Bennett
78-6697 A Mam La Hoa Hwy.
Holua Loa, HI 96725
Phone: 808-322-3375
Fax: 808-322-2664

Mil Bodron Design
2801 West Lemmon Avenue,
Suite 201
Dallas, TX 75204
Phone: 214-871-7588
Fax: 214-871-7587

Bill Booziotis
Booziotis & Co.
2400 A Empire Central Drive
Dallas, TX 75235
Phone: 214-350-5051
Fax: 214-350-5849

George Brook-Kothlow &
Associates
P.O. Box AD
Carmel, CA 93921
Phone: 408-659-4596
Fax: 408-659-4596

Lewis Butler
Butler Armsden Architects
524 2nd Street
San Francisco, CA 94107
Phone: 415-495-5495
Fax: 415-495-3203

Dahlin Group
2671 Crow Canyon Drive
San Ramone, CA 94583
Phone: 510-837-8286
Fax: 510-837-2543

Richard Drummond Davis
4310 Westside Drive, Suite H
Dallas, TX 75209
Phone: 214-521-8763
Fax: 214-522-7674

Joe Esherick
EHDD
2789 25th Street,
3rd Floor
San Francisco, CA 94110
Phone: 415-285-9193
Fax: 415-285-3866

Estudio Arthur de Mattos
Casas Ltda
Alameda Ministro Rocha
Azevedo, 1052
Sao Paulo, Sao Paulo
01410-002 Brazil
Phone: 011-55-11-282-6311
Fax: 011-55-11-282-6608

Stan Field
3631 Evergreen Drive
Palo Alto, CA 94303
Phone: 415-462-9554
Fax: 415-462-9557

Fleischman/Garcia Architects
324 Hyde Park Avenue,
Suite 300
Tampa, FL 33606
Phone: 813-251-4400
Fax: 813-251-1994

Dan Fletcher
Fletcher + Hardoin
769 Pacific Street
Monterey, CA 93940
Phone: 408-373-5855
Fax: 408-373-5889

Gary Francis & Associates
P.O. Box 2129
Park City, UT 84060
Phone: 801-649-7168
Fax: 801-649-5327

David Gast and Associates
1746 Union Street
San Francisco, CA 94123
Phone: 415-885-2946
Fax: 415-885-2808

Charles J. Grebmeier, ASID
Grebmeier-Roy Design
1298 Sacramento Street
San Francisco, CA 94108
Phone: 415-931-1088
Fax: 415-373-5409

David Hale, AIA
256 Sutter Street, #500
San Francisco, CA 94108
Phone: 415-982-1216
Fax: 415-982-0820

Holly Hall
Booziotis & Co.
2400 A Empire Central Drive
Dallas, TX 75235
Phone: 214-350-5051
Fax: 214-350-5849

Michael Helm
200 7th Avenue, #110
Santa Cruz, CA 95062
Phone: 408-476-5386
Fax: 408-476-2025

J. B. Johnson Arquiteto
Rio Volga 17-6
DF 06500 Mexico
Phone: 011-525-514-7529
Fax: 011-525-514-7529

Steve Johnson
Roeder-Johnson Corp.
655 Skyway, Suite 130
San Carlos, CA 94074
Phone: 415-802-1852
Fax: 415-593-5515

Sid Del Mar Leach, ASID
Classic Design Associates
288 Butterfield Road
San Anselmo, CA 94960
Phone: 415-454-3733

Vasco Andrade Lopes
Luiz Fernando Rocco
Arquitetos Associados S/C
Rua Mandari, 465-A
Sao Paulo, Sao Paulo
01457-020 Brazil
Phone: 011-55-11-814-6963
Fax: 011-55-11-814-6963

David Ludwig
Jared Polsky and Associates
469-B Magnolia Avenue
Larkspur, CA 94939
Phone: 415-927-1156
Fax: 415-927-0847

Richard Luke Architects
2605 South Decatur Boulevard
Las Vegas, NV 89102
Phone: 702-876-2520
Fax: 702-876-2407

William David Martin &
Associates
P.O. Box 2053
Monterey, CA 93940
Phone: 408-373-7101
Fax: 408-373-4748

Anthony Ngai, AIA
A. K. Ngai & Associates
11678 Laurelcrest Drive
Studio City, CA 91604
Phone: 818-763-5567

Alan Ohashi
Ohashi Design Studio
5739 Presley Avenue
Berkeley, CA 94618
Phone: 510-652-8840
Fax: 510-652-8604

Albert Pastine Architect
1183 Shotwell
San Francisco, CA 94119
Phone: 415-826-9292
Fax: 415-826-9298

Richard Perlstein, AIA
Jared Polsky and Associates
469-B Magnolia Avenue
Larkspur, CA 94939
Phone: 415-927-1156
Fax: 415-927-0847

Dan Phipps & Associates
1031 Post Street
San Francisco, CA 94109
Phone: 415-776-1606
Fax: 415-776-3972

Jared Polsky and Associates
469-B Magnolia Avenue
Larkspur, CA 94939
Phone: 415-927-1156
Fax: 415-927-0847

Luiz Fernando Rocco
Arquitetos Associados S/C
Rua Mandari, 465-A
Sao Paulo, Sao Paulo
01457-020 Brazil
Phone: 011-55-11-814-6963
Fax: 011-55-11-814-6963

Mary Ann Schicketanz
Carver & Schicketanz
P.O. Box 2684
Carmel, CA 93921
Phone: 408-624-2304
Fax: 408-624-0364

Richard Sherer
Lakeside Development
1535 West Market Street
Mequon, WI 53092
Phone: 414-241-2300
Fax: 414-241-2310

George Sinclair
Sinclair & Associates, Inc.
15 North Ellsworth Avenue,
Suite 100
San Mateo, CA 94401
Phone: 415-348-6865
Fax: 415-348-5062

David Allen Smith Architect
444 Pearl Street, Suite B2
Monterey, CA 93940
Phone: 408-373-7337
Fax: 408-373-1668

Charles Southall
Moore Andersson Architects
1801 North Lamar, #100
Austin, TX 78701
Phone: 512-476-5780
Fax: 512-476-0858

Gordon Stein
Stein & Associates
49858 San Juan Avenue
Palm Desert, CA 92260
Phone: 760-568-3696
Fax: 760-836-1896

Eric Stine Architect Inc.
1-1864 West 1st Avenue
Vancouver, BC V6J 1G5
Canada
Phone: 604-732-4545
Fax: 604-736-9493

Ron Sutton
Sutton-Suzuki
39 Forrest Street
Mill Valley, CA 94941
Phone: 415-456-1656
Fax: 415-457-5483

Candida Tabet
Mantovani & Tabet Com. de
Moveis Ltda
Rua Medeiros de
Albuquerque, 23
Sao Paulo, Sao Paulo
05436-060 Brazil
Phone: 011-55-11-211-0418
Fax: 011-55-11-211-3910

Seiji Tanaka
Yoshimura Architects &
Associates
28 Kamimiyanomae-Cho
Shishigatani, Sakyo-Ku
Kyoto, Kyoto 606
Japan
Phone: 011-81-075-771-6071
Fax: 011-81-075-761-5937

Mark Thomas & Associates
444 Spear Street
San Francisco, CA 94105
Phone: 415-495-2778
Fax: 415-495-3336

Duncan Todd
T^2
414 Mason Street, Suite 702
San Francisco, CA 95102
Phone: 415-362-7670
Fax: 415-362-7672

Ravi Varma
RNM
4611 Teller Avenue, #100
Newport Beach, CA 92660
Phone: 714-262-0908

Lee von Hasseln
P.O. Box 213
Pebble Beach, CA 93953
Phone: 408-625-6467

Stephen Wilmot
4114 El Bosque Drive
Pebble Beach, CA 93953
Phone: 408-625-5399

Interior Designers

Eugene Anthony & Associates
2408 Fillmore Street
San Francisco, CA 94115
Phone: 415-567-9575
Fax: 415-567-9590

Lynn AugStein, ASID, CID
LAS Design
3 Wolfback Terrace
Sausalito, CA 94965
Phone: 415-332-3323
Fax: 415-332-1342

Sheron Bailey
Design Ideas
12390 Avenue 18½
Chowchilla, CA 93610
Phone: 209-665-4515
Fax: 209-665-3645

Lou Ann Bauer
Bauer Interior Design
239 Broderick Street
San Francisco, CA 94117
Phone: 415-621-7262
Fax: 415-621-3661

Hamlet C. "Lucky" Bennett
78-6697 A Mam La Hoa Hwy.
Holua Loa, HI 96725
Phone: 808-322-3375
Fax: 808-322-2664

Mil Bodron Design
2801 West Lemmon Avenue,
Suite 201
Dallas, TX 75204
Phone: 214-871-7588
Fax: 214-871-7587

Sandra Brown Interiors Inc.
537 Sycamore Valley Rd. West
Danville, CA 94526
Phone: 510-837-1370
Fax: 510-837-6514

Kathleen Buoymaster Inc.
6933 La Jolla Boulevard
La Jolla, CA 92037
Phone: 619-456-2850
Fax: 619-456-0672

Sherrill Bushfield
Raintree Design
15957 Marine Drive
White Rock, British Columbia
Canada V4B 1G1
Phone: 604-538-2216
Fax: 604-538-6614

Albert Carey, ASID
Acorn Kitchens and Baths
4640 Telegraph Avenue
Oakland, CA 94609
Phone: 510-547-6581
Fax: 510-547-2815

Carla Carstens' Designs
1 Timber View Road
Soquel, CA 95073
Phone: 408-462-4775
Fax: 408-462-2209

Jere Cavanaugh
Rio Volga 17-6
DF 06500 Mexico
Phone: 011-525-514-7529
Fax: 011-525-514-7529

Diane Chapman Interiors
3380 Washington Street
San Francisco, CA 94118
Phone: 415-346-2373
Fax: 415-346-5264

Peggy Chestnut Interior
Design
c/o Maryl Development
755751 Kuakini Highway,
Suite 101A
Kailua-Kona, HI 96740
Phone: 808-329-9370

Debbie Collins, ASID
Ruth Soforenko & Associates
137 Forest Avenue
Palo Alto, CA 94301
Phone: 415-326-5448
Fax: 415-326-5539

James Connelly Interiors
5621 North Lake Drive
Milwaukee, WI 53217
Phone: 414-332-0610

Winifred Dell'Ario
Design Dell'Ario
P.O. Box 3200
Half Moon Bay, CA 94019
Phone: 415-726-7122
Fax: 415-726-1877

Roger C. Duffala
DVT Design Group
1200 West Platt Street,
Suite 201
Tampa, FL 33606
Phone: 813-253-6068
Fax: 813-254-1603

Estudio Arthur de Mattos
Casas Ltda
Alameda Ministro Rocha
Azevedo, 1052
Sao Paulo, Sao Paulo
01410-002 Brazil
Phone: 011-55-11-282-6311
Fax: 011-55-11-282-6608

Cheri Etchelecu Interior
Design
9400 North Central
Expressway, #1605
Dallas, TX 75231-5045
Phone: 214-369-7486
Fax: 214-369-3691

Toby Flax Interior Design
Studio
444 DeHaro Street, #122
San Francisco, CA 94107
Phone: 415-252-8184
Fax: 415-252-9006

Charles J. Grebmeier, ASID
Grebmeier-Roy Design
1298 Sacramento Street
San Francisco, CA 94108
Phone: 415-931-1088
Fax: 415-373-5409

Russell Greey
Brant & Greey
1110 East Missouri
Phoenix, AZ 85014
Phone: 602-222-8848

Charles Paxton Gremillion
Loyd-Paxton Inc.
3636 Maple Avenue
Dallas, TX 75219
Phone: 214-521-1521
Fax: 214-522-4438

Casey Grenier
Correll Design
1811 Los Altos Drive
San Mateo, CA 94402
Phone: 415-341-3280

Courtney Griffith Interiors
300 Summit Drive
Corte Madera, CA 94925
Phone: 415-924-5699
Fax: 415-924-5699

David Hale
256 Sutter Street, #500
San Francisco, CA 94108
Phone: 415-982-1216
Fax: 415-982-0820

Jessica Hall Associates
1301 6th Street, Suite G
San Francisco, CA 94107-2222
Phone: 415-552-9923
Fax: 415-552-9963

Phil Hardoin
Fletcher + Hardoin
769 Pacific Street
Monterey, CA 93940
Phone: 408-373-5855
Fax: 408-373-5889

Jerry Hettinger
J. Hettinger Interiors
200 Hartz Avenue
Danville, CA 94526
Phone: 510-820-9336
Fax: 510-820-9414

Barbara Jacobs Interior Design
12340 Saratoga-Sunnyvale Rd.
Saratoga, CA 95070
Phone: 408-446-2225
Fax: 408-446-2607

Allen Kirsch Interior Design
3131 Turtle Creek, Suite 820
Dallas, TX 75219
Phone: 214-526-5496
Fax: 214-526-5498

Bobbie Dawn Lander
3602 Beltline Rd.
Sunnyvale, TX 75182
Phone: 972-226-2701

Lorraine Lazowick, ASID
5132 Redbud Grove Lane
Roseville, CA 95747
Phone: 916-771-4601
Fax: 916-771-4601

Rhonda Luongo, ASID, CCID
Devlyn Corp.
205 Crystal Springs Center,
Suite 104
San Mateo, CA 94402
Phone: 415-579-2594
Fax: 415-579-2594

Valera W. Lyles
P.O. Box 223513
Carmel, CA 93922

William Manly Associates, Inc.
301 North Water Street
Milwaukee, WI 53201
Phone: 414-291-5200

William David Martin, AIA
P.O. Box 2053
Monterey, CA 93940
Phone: 408-373-7101
Fax: 408-373-4708

Lawrence Masnada Design
1745 20th Street
San Francisco, CA 94107
Phone: 415-641-8364
Fax: 415-641-0136

Anne Maurice
1456 Jefferson Street
San Francisco, CA 94123
Phone: 415-885-4022

Donald Maxcy, ASID
Maxcy Design
Lincoln between 7th & 8th
P.O. Box 5507
Carmel, CA 93921
Phone: 408-625-5081
Fax: 408-625-5031

Tina Messner
4418 Smoke Tree Lane
Concord, CA 94521
Phone: 510-682-9656

Frederick Miley Designs
345 Vermont
San Francisco, CA 94103
Phone: 415-931-5605
Fax: 415-626-9036

Bob Miller
Flegels
870 Santa Cruz Avenue
Menlo Park, CA 94025
Phone: 415-326-9661
Fax: 415-326-0869

John Newcomb
P.O. Box 671
Carmel, CA 93921
Phone: 408-624-9637

Alan Ohashi
Ohashi Design Studio
5739 Presley Avenue
Berkeley, CA 94618
Phone: 510-652-8840
Fax: 510-652-8604

Joan Malter Osburn, Allied
Member, ASID
Osburn Design
200 Kansas Street, Suite 208
San Francisco, CA 94103
Phone: 415-487-2333
Fax: 415-487-2345

Joe Prados
Laurie Smith Design
Associates
407 B East 6th Street, #204
Austin, TX 78701
Phone: 512-477-7683
Fax: 512-477-7864

Helen C. Reuter
Details, Inc.
1250 Jones Street, #1102
San Francisco, CA 94109
Phone: 415-921-3236
Fax: 415-921-0139

Marilyn Riding Design
12340 Saratoga-Sunnyvale
Road, Suite 2-3
Saratoga, CA 95070
Phone: 408-446-3166
Fax: 408-446-2607

Luiz Fernando Rocco
Arquitetos Associados S/C
Ltda
Rua Mandari, 465-A
Sao Paulo, Sao Paulo
01457-020 Brazil
Phone: 011-55-11-814-6963
Fax: 011-55-11-814-6963

Craig A. Roeder & Associates
3829 North Hall Street
Dallas, TX 75219
Phone: 214-528-2300
Fax: 214-521-2300

Joseph Ruggiero & Associates
4512 Louise Avenue
Encino, CA 91316
Phone: 818-783-9257

Priscilla Sanchez Interiors
444 De Haro Street, Suite 101
San Francisco, CA 94017
Phone: 415-864-7766
Fax: 415-864-1715

Mary Ann Schicketanz
Carver & Schicketanz
P.O. Box 2684
Carmel, CA 93921
Phone: 408-624-2304
Fax: 408-624-0364

John Schneider Design
P.O. Box 1457
Pebble Beach, CA 93953
Phone: 408-649-8221
Fax: 408-655-1093

April Sheldon Design
477 Bryant Street
San Francisco, CA 94107
Phone: 415-541-7773
Fax: 415-284-0274

Joanne Sheridan
Sturgeon Interiors
229 West Bender Road
Milwaukee, WI 53217
Phone: 414-964-8288

Lindy Smallwood Interiors
111 F Town & Country Dr.
Danville, CA 94526
Phone: 510-837-1312
Fax: 510-837-0499

Ruth Soforenko & Associates
137 Forest Avenue
Palo Alto, CA 94301
Phone: 415-326-5448
Fax: 415-326-5539

Victoria Stone Interiors
893 Noe Street
San Francisco, CA 94114
Phone: 415-826-0904
Fax: 415-826-1893

Suzman Design Associates
233 Douglas Street
San Francisco, CA 94114
Phone: 415-252-0111
Fax: 415-861-6163

Candida Tabet
Mantovani & Tabet Com. de
Moveis Ltda
Rua Medeiros de
Albuquerque, 23
Sao Paulo, Sao Paulo
05436-060 Brazil
Phone: 011-55-11-211-0418
Fax: 011-55-11-211-3910

Seiji Tanaka
Yoshimura Architects &
Associates
14-22, 1-Chome, Akasaka
Chuo-Ku
Fukuoka, Fukuoka 810
Japan
Phone: 092-715-6412
Fax: 092-715-6413

Loyd Ray Taylor
Loyd-Paxton Inc.
3636 Maple Avenue
Dallas, TX 75219
Phone: 214-521-1521
Fax: 214-522-4438

Jacqueline Thornton
Jacqueline & Associates
928 South Valley View
Las Vegas, NV 98107
Phone: 702-877-9347
Fax: 702-877-3957

Stella Tuttle, ASID, CID
Tuttle & Associates
4155 El Camino Way, #2
Palo Alto, CA 94306
Phone: 415-857-1171
Fax: 415-857-1173

Jim Wallen
Acorn Kitchens and Baths
4640 Telegraph Avenue
Oakland, CA 94609
Phone: 510-547-6581
Fax: 510-547-2815

Cathy Wentz Interior Design
85 Stevenson Lane
Atherton, CA 94027
Phone: 415-327-7009
Fax: 415-327-7007

Dudley Williams
Wheatman & Associates
1933 Union Street
San Francisco, CA 94123
Phone: 415-346-8300
Fax: 415-771-8652

Christian Wright
Robert Hering & Associates
151 Vermont Street, #7
San Francisco, CA 94103
Phone: 415-863-4144
Fax: 415-863-4152

Lighting Designers

Lynn AugStein, ASID, CID
LAS Design
3 Wolfback Terrace
Sausalito, CA 94127
Phone: 415-332-3323
Fax: 415-332-1342

Axiom Design Inc.
56718 Sonoma Drive
Pleasanton, CA 94566
Phone: 510-462-2300
Fax: 510-462-8948

Bradley A. Bouch
Spectrum Lighting Design
6767 West Tropicana, #208
Las Vegas, NV 89103
Phone: 702-248-1057
Fax: 702-248-1067

Barbara Bouyea, IALD, IES
Bouyea & Associates
3811 Turtle Creek Boulevard,
Suite 1010
Dallas, TX 75219
Phone: 241-520-6580
Fax: 241-520-6581

Sandra Brown Interiors Inc.
537 Sycamore Valley Rd. West
Danville, CA 94526
Phone: 510-837-1370
Fax: 510-837-6514

Kathleen Buoymaster
6933 La Jolla Boulevard
La Jolla, CA 92037
Phone: 619-456-2850

Fax: 619-456-0672
Linda Ferry, IES, ASID
Architectural Illumination
P.O. Box 2690
Monterey, CA 93942
Phone: 408-649-3711
Fax: 408-375-5897

Becca Foster Lighting Design
27 South Park
San Francisco, CA 94107
Phone: 415-541-0370
Fax: 415-957-5856

Sarah J. Gibson, IESNA, IALD
Archillume Lightning Design
3701 Executive Center Dr., #150
Austin, TX 78731
Phone: 512-346-1386
Fax: 512-346-1387

Janis Huston, IES, IALD
Sand Dollar—A Lighting
Design Co.
932 Tsawwassen Beach
South Delta, BC V4M 2J3
Canada
Phone: 604-943-5641
Fax: 604-943-8783

Duane Johnson, IESNA
Artistic Lighting Corp.
767 Lincoln Avenue,
Suite 8
San Rafael, CA 94901
Phone: 415-456-1656

Fax: 415-457-5483
Cynthia Bolton Karasik
The Lighting Group
200 Pine Street
San Francisco, CA 94109
Phone: 415-989-3446
Fax: 415-989-40056

Steven L. Klein
Standard Electric Supply Co.
222 North Emmber Lane
Milwaukee, WI 53233
Phone: 800-776-8222
Fax: 414-272-8111

Anna Kondolf Lighting
Design
94 Toyon Drive
Fairfax, CA 94930
Phone: 415-456-5472
Fax: 415-456-5473

Alan Lindsley
Lindsley-McCoy Architecture
& Lighting
221 Main Street, Suite 940
San Francisco, CA 94105

Kousaku Matsumoto, IEI
Kitani Design Associates
City Pole 4-5, 4-Chome
Awajimachi, Chuo-Ku
Osaka, Osaka 541
Japan
Phone: 011-81-06-232-1641
Fax: 011-81-06-232-1642

Donald Maxcy, ASID
Maxcy Design
Lincoln between 7th & 8th
P.O. Box 5507
Carmel, CA 93921
Phone: 408-625-5081
Fax: 408-625-5031

Ahnalisa Moore Design
280 Grove Acre
Pacific Grove, CA 93950
Phone: 408-649-3925
Fax: 408-372-3138

Catherine Ng, IES
Light Source Design Group
1246 18th Street
San Francisco, CA 94107
Phone: 415-626-1210
Fax: 415-626-1821

Terry Ohm
Ohm Lighting and Design
601 Minnesota Street
San Francisco, CA 94107
Phone: 415-641-1161
Fax: 415-252-5958

Guinter Parschalk
RDX-Radix Comercial Ltda
Rua Fernando Falcao, 121
Sao Paulo, Sao Paulo
03180-001 Brazil
Phone: 011-55-11-291-0944
Fax: 011-55-11-608-2257

David W. Patton, IES
Intelectric
3333 Kimberly Way
San Mateo, CA 94403
Phone: 415-574-2371
Fax: 415-286-0639

Craig A. Roeder & Associates
3829 North Hall Street
Dallas, TX 75219
Phone: 214-528-2300
Fax: 214-521-2300

Sherry Scott, ASID
Design Lab
601 4th Street, #125
San Francisco, CA 94107
Phone: 415-974-1934

Michael Souter, ASID
Luminae Souter
1740 Army Street
2nd Floor
San Francisco, CA 94124
Phone: 415-285-2622
Fax: 415-285-5718

Charles K. Thompson, AIA,
IESNA, IALD
Archillume Lighting Design
3701 Executive Center Dr., #150
Austin, TX 78731
Phone: 512-346-1386
Fax: 512-346-1387

Randall Whitehead, IALD,
ASID Affiliate
Light Source Design Group
1246 18th Street
San Francisco, CA 94107
Phone: 415-626-1210
Fax: 415-626-1821

Alfredo Zaparolli
Techlinea Design Associates
2325 3rd Street
San Francisco, CA 94107
Phone: 415-863-7773
Fax: 415-621-0467

Photographers

Russell Abraham Photography
60 Federal Street, Suite 303
San Francisco, CA 94107
Phone: 415-896-6400
Fax: 415-896-6402

Dennis Anderson Photography
48 Lucky Drive
Greenbrae, CA 94904
Phone: 415-927-3530
Fax: 415-927-2659

Yoshihisa Araki
Atelier Fukumoto Co.
301 Crest Shinsaibashi 4-12-9
Minamisenba, Chuo-Ku
Osaka, Osaka 542 Japan
Phone: 011-81-06-245-4680
Fax: 011-81-06-245-4682

Paul Bardagjy Photography
4111 Marathon Boulevard
Austin, TX 78756
Phone: 512-452-9636
Fax: 512-452-6425

Robert Bengtson Photography
8A Ridge Avenue
Mill Valley, CA 94941
Phone: 415-380-8486
Fax: 415-380-8486

Jeff Blanton Photography
5515 South Orange Avenue
Orlando, FL 32809
Phone: 407-851-7279
Fax: 407-857-7272

Michael Bruk
Photo/Graphics
731 Florida Street
Studio 201
San Francisco, CA 94110
Phone: 415-824-8600
Fax: 415-824-8375

John Canham
Quadra Focus
588 Waite Avenue
Sunnyvale, CA 94086
Phone: 408-739-1465
Fax: 408-739-9117

John Casado Photography
477 Bryant Street
San Francisco, CA 94107
Phone: 415-284-0164
Fax: 415-284-0274

Dave Chawla Associates
P.O. Box 26931
Las Vegas, NV 89126
Phone: 702-253-6306

Robert Ames Cook
Photography
809 Hickory Highland Drive
Antioch, TN 37013
Phone: 615-591-3270
Fax: 615-591-0937

Jay Graham Photography
P.O. Box 1607
San Anselmo, CA 94960
Phone: 415-459-3839

Philip Harvey Photography
911 Minna Street
San Francisco, CA 94103
Phone: 415-861-2188
Fax: 415-861-2091

Mark F. Heffron
Heffoto
P.O. Box 700
Milwaukee, WI 53202
Phone: 414-962-0719

Douglas Johnson Photography
P.O. Box 984
Danville, CA 94526
Phone: 510-837-4482
Fax: 510-837-7734

Muffy Kibbey Photography
3036 Hillegass Avenue
Berkeley, CA 94705
Phone: 510-549-1115
Fax: 510-549-1199

David Livingston
Photography
1036 Erica Road
Mill Valley, CA 94941
Phone: 415-383-0898
Fax: 415-383-0897

John Martin Photography
68 Ashton Avenue
San Francisco, CA 94112
Phone: 415-337-7408

Ira Montgomery Photography
2406 Converse
Dallas, TX 75207
Phone: 214-638-7288
Fax: 214-638-7980

Mary E. Nichols
232 N. Arden Boulevard
Los Angeles, CA 90004
Phone: 213-871-0770
Fax: 213-871-0775

Andres Otero
Blick Producoes
Av. Higienopolis, 578/87
Sao Paulo, Sao Paulo
01238-000 Brazil
Phone: 011-55-11-824-0779
Fax: 011-55-11-824-0779

Gary Otte
Foto: Otte Photographer
21-1551 Johnston Street
Granville Island
Vancouver, BC U6H 3R9
Canada
Phone: 604-681-8421

Eric Oxendorf Studio
1442 North Franklin Place
Milwaukee, WI 53202
Phone: 414-273-0654
Fax: 414-273-1759

Tuca Reines Estudio
Fotografico Ltda
Rua Emanoel Kant, 58
Sao Paulo, Sao Paulo
04536-050 Brazil
Phone: 011-55-11-3061-9127
Fax: 011-55-11-852-8735

Kenneth Rice Photography
456 61st Street
Oakland, CA 94103
Phone: 510-652-1752
Fax: 510-658-4355

Sharon Risedorph
Photography
761 Clementina Street
San Francisco, CA 94103
Phone: 415-431-5851

Fax: 415-431-2537

Cesar Rubio
2565 Third Street
San Francisco, CA 94107
Phone: 415-550-6369

Douglas A. Salin Photography
647 Joost Avenue
San Francisco, CA 94127
Phone: 415-584-3322
Pager: 415-227-6600

Ron Starr Photography
4104 24th Street, #358
San Francisco, CA 94114
Phone: 415-541-7732
Fax: 415-285-9518

John Sutton Photography
8 Main Street
Point San Quentin, CA 94964
Phone: 415-258-8100
Fax: 415-258-1167

Toshiya Toyoda
Toyoda Photo Studio
1-3611 Sakuraoka, Shime-cho
Kasuyagun, Fukuoka 811-ZZ
Japan 811-22
Phone: 011-092-935-7987

John Vaughan Photography
5242 Reedley Way
Hayward, CA 94546
Phone: 510-481-9814
Fax: 510-481-9238

Alan Weintraub Photography
1832 A Mason Street
San Francisco, CA 94114
Phone: 415-553-8191
Fax: 415-553-8192

Tom Wyatt
Sunset Publishing Co.
80 Willow Road
Menlo Park, CA 94025
Phone: 415-321-3600

Eric A. Zepeda
4X5
1451 Stevenson Street, Studio A
San Francisco, CA 94103
Phone: 415-558-9691

Scott Zimmerman
Architectural Photography
P.O. Box 289
Heber City, UT 84032
Phone: 801-279-2757
Fax: 801-654-5090